Propertius, Tibullus and Ovid:
A Selection of Love Poetry

The following titles are available from Bloomsbury for the OCR specifications in Latin and Greek, first teaching September 2016

Cicero *Pro Milone*: A Selection, with introduction by Lynn Fotheringham and commentary notes and vocabulary by Robert West

Ovid *Heroides*: A Selection, with introduction, commentary notes and vocabulary by John Godwin

Propertius, Tibullus and Ovid: A Selection of Love Poetry, with introduction, commentary notes and vocabulary by Anita Nikkanen

Seneca Letters: A Selection, with introduction, commentary notes and vocabulary by Eliot Maunder

Tacitus *Annals* I: A Selection, with introduction by Roland Mayer and commentary notes and vocabulary by Katharine Radice

Virgil *Aeneid* VIII: A Selection, with introduction, commentary notes and vocabulary by Keith Maclennan

Virgil *Aeneid* X: A Selection, with introduction, commentary notes and vocabulary by Christopher Tanfield

OCR Anthology for Classical Greek GCSE, covering the prescribed texts by Homer, Herodotus, Euripides, Lucian, Plato and Plutarch, edited by Judith Affleck and Clive Letchford

OCR Anthology for Classical Greek AS and A-level, covering the prescribed texts by Aristophanes, Homer, Plato, Sophocles, Thucydides and Xenophon, with introduction, commentary notes and vocabulary by Malcolm Campbell, Rob Colborn, Frederica Daniele, Ben Gravell, Sarah Harden, Steven Kennedy, Matthew McCullagh, Charlie Paterson, John Taylor and Claire Webster

Supplementary resources for these volumes can be found at www.bloomsbury.com/OCR-editions
Please type the URL into your web browser and follow the instructions to access the Companion Website. If you experience any problems, please contact Bloomsbury at academicwebsite@bloomsbury.com

Propertius, Tibullus and Ovid: A Selection of Love Poetry

Propertius *Elegies* 1.1, 1.3 and 2.14
Tibullus *Elegies* 1.1 and 1.3
Ovid *Amores* 1.1, 2.5, 2.7 and 2.8

With introduction, commentary notes and
vocabulary by Anita Nikkanen

Bloomsbury Academic
An imprint of Bloomsbury Publishing Plc

B L O O M S B U R Y
LONDON · OXFORD · NEW YORK · NEW DELHI · SYDNEY

Bloomsbury Academic

An imprint of Bloomsbury Publishing Plc

50 Bedford Square   1385 Broadway
London   New York
WC1B 3DP   NY 10018
UK   USA

www.bloomsbury.com

**BLOOMSBURY and the Diana logo are trademarks of Bloomsbury
Publishing Plc**

First published 2016

Introduction, commentary notes and vocabulary © Anita Nikkanen, 2016

Anita Nikkanen has asserted her right under the Copyright, Designs and
Patents Act, 1988, to be identified as Author of this work.

British Library Cataloguing-in-Publication Data

A catalogue record for this book is available from the British Library.

ISBN: PB: 978-1-47426-614-7
    ePub: 978-1-47426-615-4
    ePDF: 978-1-47426-616-1

Library of Congress Cataloging-in-Publication Data

A catalog record for this book is available from the Library of Congress.

Typeset by RefineCatch Limited, Bungay, Suffolk
Printed and bound in Great Britain

Contents

Preface   vii

Introduction   1

Text   35

Commentary Notes   51

Vocabulary   125

Preface

The text and notes found in this volume are designed to guide any student who has mastered Latin up to GCSE level and wishes to read a selection of Propertius's, Tibullus's and Ovid's love elegies in the original. The edition is, however, particularly designed to support students who are reading the elegies in preparation for OCR's AS or A-Level Latin examination in June 2017–19. (Please note this edition uses AS to refer indiscriminately to AS and the expected first year of A Level, i.e. Group 1.) The selections provide a representative introduction to the genre of Latin love elegy and its conventions, as well as the different styles of the three authors. While they share the themes of love elegy – most importantly, the celebration of their beloved in poetry – they each bring their own take to it.

This edition contains a detailed introduction to the context of the selected Latin love elegies and the genre and style of the elegists, supported by summaries of the poems, a glossary of rhetorical devices used in this volume and a note on metre. The text of the elegies printed here is that of Robert Maltby, *Latin Love Elegy: Selected and Edited with Introduction and Notes* (Bristol: Bristol Classical Press, 1980), with a handful of changes, which are noted in the commentary. The poems are presented here in chronological order by author, starting with Propertius and ending with Ovid, who frequently responds and alludes to his predecessors; you are, of course, free to study them in any order. The notes to the elegies themselves aim to help students bridge the gap between GCSE and AS Level Latin, and focus therefore on the harder points of grammar and word order, background information necessary for understanding the text, such as mythology or religious practices, and points of style impacting on meaning. At the end of the book is a full vocabulary list for all the words contained in the prescribed elegies, with words in OCR's Defined Vocabulary List for AS Level Latin flagged by means of an asterisk.

In the notes on the text, I offer alternative interpretations of (and so, ways of translating) phrases and words. This is in order to illustrate the multivalent meanings of the text and the poetic beauty thereby afforded, as well as the ongoing scholarly debate about the particular meaning of a detail in the text. I therefore encourage students to enjoy this beauty and, for the purposes of finding their own translation, to consider the poem for themselves and choose the translation that best matches the way they interpret the poem. Even among specialists who have spent years studying these texts, there is not always consensus, but the best argued case is the most persuasive.

I am very grateful to Alice Wright and her team at Bloomsbury, and especially to the anonymous reviewer on her team and to the OCR reviewer for the many helpful suggestions and improvements.

Anita Nikkanen

October 2015

Introduction

What is Latin love elegy?

Latin love elegy is a genre of poetry that emerged in the first century BC in Rome, amidst significant political and cultural changes as the Roman Republic gave way to imperial rule under Augustus (see further on the political context below). The genre itself was short-lived: the time period from the earliest elegies by Gallus to those of the last elegist, Ovid, spans only about forty years. The main Roman elegists are the ones focused on in this book; Propertius, Tibullus and Ovid (only very small fragments of Gallus's elegies survive, and other elegiac poems are included in what is called the Tibullan body of poetry, although not all of the poems are by him). Despite the short time period during which Latin love elegy was composed, it has its own distinguishing characteristics and conventions. Although other topics are included, a prominent feature of Latin love elegy is the relationship of the poet with his beloved mistress: as the name suggests, they are love poems, depicting the ups and downs of the relationship. Often the poems directly address the beloved: indeed, they are spoken from the subjective, first-person stance of the poet. While some express the poet's devotion to his mistress, others convey the heartbreak and jealousy when the love is not reciprocated.

In fact, it is this distinctive character of Latin love elegy that opens up the Roman world to a modern audience in a particularly accessible and, in some ways, familiar manner. Through the more subjective, first-person narrative of elegy we can really feel like we are getting to know the Romans – well, some of them – more personally. Instead of the cold, white marble statues and heroes excelling in battle or in the law courts, in elegy we meet everyday individuals with distinguishing personal characteristics, wishes, hopes and desires, to many of which we can relate more directly. While many of us moderns do not experience battlefields, epic journeys to found cities, or argue cases at law (at least not until a later age), most of us do experience and can relate to the ups and downs of a relationship and the emotions it provokes. What is more, our popular culture still deals with the same concerns: unrequited love, broken hearts and lovers' intrigues are as ever-present in the pop music and television shows today as they are in Latin elegy. Through Latin love elegy, we can not only get to know the Romans better, but also explore different ways of looking at issues that still occupy us today.

Cultural, political and literary context in Rome

Fame for Romans was achieved through a distinguished political and military career, and poetry was originally considered a low-status activity: the earliest significant writers, such as Plautus (active c. 205–184 BC) and Ennius (239–169 BC), were dependants of powerful Romans, even slaves. Full-time poets were clients, whereas members of the Roman elite, like the young Cicero (106–43 BC), might dabble in writing poetry as a form of relaxation; literary appreciation was seen as a part of being cultivated, but poetry was not a serious pursuit in itself. Insofar as literature advanced the fame of Roman citizens and so of Rome herself, it was valued. History and oratory, directly connected to public life, involved gaining a name and commemorating achievements. These, therefore, were genres in which eminent Romans could write seriously (Cato, 234–149 BC, and Cicero are prominent examples). Not surprisingly, then, genres of poetry that fulfilled the same function were valued for this gift of fame – especially grand epics commemorating the accomplishments of Romans and their ancestors.

In the late Republic, however, a new literary movement arose. In addition to poetry as a pastime, like in the case of Cicero in this period, respectable Romans began to write poetry with pride. Since they were of independent means, they could write to please themselves and their friends, not to satisfy the tastes of a patron or a popular audience. They rejected traditionally valued subjects and genres, such as historical epic on events of public significance, in favour of smaller-scale poems focusing on personal experience and emotion. Love, especially when it violated social norms, became a seriously treated theme. Stylistic refinement as well as a small refined audience were preferred to great public appeal. In fact, these Romans looked to the Hellenistic poets of Alexandria, and especially Callimachus as an important model for style, subject matter and verse-forms: he had championed smaller-scale, learned poetry aimed at an equally learned audience. The best known member of this generation of Roman poets, often called *novi poetae* ('new poets') or *neoterics*, is Catullus. He was from a good provincial family and well connected in Rome (a friend of the eminent orator Calvus, he had at least some contact with Julius Caesar); he was not a dependent of an eminent Roman patron. Among his poems are ones describing his tumultuous relationship with a woman he calls Lesbia, whom Apuleius identifies with Clodia. If this identification is true and she is the Clodia Metelli whom we know from Cicero's *Pro Caelio*, she was a married aristocratic lady. That would have made the relationship illicit by the society's norms. Either way, though, the name Lesbia, 'woman from Lesbos', would suggest to a Roman reader a courtesan from the Greek island, as well as its famous poetess, Sappho. Whoever Catullus's mistress is, she is a figure of love, sophistication and poetry. Although Catullus did on occasion use the elegiac metre and write about love, he was not, strictly speaking, a love elegist. However, his influence on Propertius, Tibullus and Ovid is obvious, and in many ways his contributions to the developments in Latin love poetry paved the way for the emergence of love elegy. Some of his poems indeed share much with especially Propertius (e.g. Cat. 66–8).

Times changed once again, however: the end of the Republic was marked by civil wars and the rise of Octavian (the future emperor Augustus) into power. After his victory over Mark Antony at Actium in 31 BC had established Octavian in sole power, he restored the Republican institutions: there were still senators and consuls, the highest title that could be held for only a year at a time. However, power became increasingly concentrated in the hands of one man. Octavian held the consulship himself continuously from 31 to 23 BC, often together with a close associate, and his influence extended to much of the political system even beyond that date. The poets, such as Virgil, Gallus and Horace, were personally affected by the political changes and wars (see e.g. the references to the devastating effects of the land confiscations in Virgil's *Eclogues*). Gallus was himself directly involved, and combined a military career with composing poetry: he took part in Octavian's Egyptian campaign and was made the first Prefect in the new province. After Gallus boastfully celebrated his achievements with monuments in Egypt, however, he was recalled to Rome, banished from the house and provinces of Octavian on account of his insolent pride, indicted in the senate and eventually forced to commit suicide in 27–26 BC. In the new political setting, artistic patronage replaced the independence that Catullus had enjoyed: Virgil and Horace both belonged to the circle of Maecenas, Octavian's right hand man. Their poetry combines an approach to political issues with a private, personal perspective, even when touching on public events, and they resist heroic epic in favour of a lighter genre (later in his career, however, Virgil does embrace epic with the *Aeneid*). They adapt the *recusatio*, a polite refusal to write epic to celebrate the exploits of a notable patron, from the model of Callimachus *Aitia* 1.1 (e.g. Virgil *Eclogue* 6, Horace *Odes* 4.15, and with some variation *Odes* 1.6 and Virgil *Georgics* 3.1–48, where he does promise epic to celebrate Octavian, but not now, only later – a promise he comes to fulfil with the *Aeneid*). Furthermore, they, like Catullus, observe the Callimachean aesthetic of refined, learned poetry. They are acutely aware of the role of poetry in conferring fame, and it is through their works, rather than the traditional political or military career, that they seek to fulfil their ambitions: for them, the poem can be a monument as powerful as a triumphal arch in conferring a lasting name – but, for example in Horace *Odes* 3.3, it is for the poet, not the patron.

Of this generation of poets, Cornelius Gallus is particularly relevant to the development of love elegy. Although only small fragments of his poetry survive, they suffice to confirm his position as originator of the genre as we know it from Propertius, Tibullus and Ovid; he was clearly an important influence on them (see Ovid *Tristia* 4.10.53–4, where Ovid lines up the four elegists in succession). He wrote in elegiac couplets and the occurrence of the word *domina*, 'mistress', in his surviving verses suggests that he initiated the standard scenario of *servitium amoris*, where the beloved female dominates over an enslaved lover. What is more, his four books of love elegies, apparently titled *Amores*, 'Loves', are addressed to Lycoris. This name is taken to be a pseudonym for a freedwoman actress called Cytheris, a mistress of Mark Antony (or so we are told by the early commentator Servius). In Virgil *Eclogue* 10, Gallus features as suffering from unrequited yet devoted love for Lycoris, who has left him to follow another man. His poetry developed the relationship with a woman under a pseudonym that we find in Catullus decidedly towards the formalized genre of love elegy that the three younger elegists inherited.

Propertius, Tibullus and Ovid, while overlapping temporally with Virgil, Horace and Gallus, belong to a generation younger than theirs. They were probably too young to have themselves been involved in the civil wars, though Propertius's and Tibullus's families seem to have lost property as a result, and their poems show acute awareness of the suffering the war caused. Ovid, younger still, not only did not experience the civil wars, but for him, the principate under Octavian/ Augustus was already in place by the time he came to Rome. They all seem to have been of equestrian rank (originally 'cavalry' or 'knights', but by this time they were generally businessmen or civil servants, a part of the wealthy upper class, freeborn and land-owning), and of relatively independent means.

Most of what we know of the biographical details of these three Latin elegists comes from their own poetry, and is therefore best taken with a pinch of salt. Insofar as we may trust it, though, from Propertius himself we learn that he was born around 55–48 BC at or near Assisi in Umbria and that his father died when he was young. One of his kinsmen died in the Perusine War (possibly also the reason for his father's death around that time) and his family's estates were affected by the land confiscations of 41–40 BC. It seems that his circumstances remained comfortable nevertheless. His mother intended him for a career in law, but when Propertius came to Rome, he became associated with poets and that became his chosen career, as well.

His first book of elegies was published in 30–29 BC, and in it, he names several friends, such as fellow poets Bassus and Ponticus. In the first poem (and others, including the last one) he addresses Tullus, a young member of an upper class family and the nephew of L. Volcatius Tullus, consul in 33 BC with Octavian, but there is no mention of Maecenas. The prime patron of the Augustan regime does appear in 2.1, where Propertius declines to write about Octavian's or Maecenas's successes. It seems therefore that his first book of elegies brought him to the attention of Maecenas and he was involved with his circle of poets, though his poems show no close friendship between him and Virgil, Horace or Tibullus. Propertius does not seem to have been indebted to a powerful patron in the manner of Virgil and Horace, however, and maintained financial and political independence, as evidenced by the attitude of his poems that refer to current affairs and people. No one could be entirely free of the political realities of the time, however, and even in his case political irreverence becomes less obvious as pressures from above strengthen over time. His last datable poem shows that he was still alive in 16 BC (4.11, a funeral elegy to a Cornelia who died that year) but dead by 2 AD (Ovid includes him among writers of the past in *Remedia Amoris* 764).

In all, we have four books of elegies by Propertius. The first focuses on Cynthia and the poet's relationship with her, and seems to have been circulated independently even after the publication of further collections of elegies. They draw on Hellenistic poetry, especially the epigrammatists, and probably on Gallus among the Roman poets. Indebtedness to Catullus's Lesbia poems comes through in the emotional intensity and upheavals, as well as the attention to the lover's feelings and the use of mythology. The second book of elegies, completed around 26–25 BC (which some think is in its current form a conflation of two distinct books, given its much greater length and other considerations) still continues with Cynthia and themes already present in the first book, but the range of themes becomes wider. Cynthia is named in only 12 of the 34 poems, and becomes a more stereotyped figure, while the tensions of the relationship, from extremes of jealousy to joy (as we see in 2.14), are explored, but also treated with more detachment and irony. Propertius becomes more explicit about his poetic allegiances and ambitions; these themes gain even more prominence in book 3 (completed around 23–33 BC), where Callimachus and Philitas are named influences (3.1 and 3.3). That book is Propertius's most varied collection when it comes to subject matter, and Cynthia is named in only the last two of the 25 poems. They mark the end of the affair and Propertius's role as a lover-poet. In the fourth book, Propertius turns to aetiological poems in the manner of Callimachus's *Aitia*, elegies explaining the origins of festivals, cults and names. But Propertius writes about decidedly *Roman* origins – indeed, he there claims the title of a Roman Callimachus (4.1.64). Love is still a theme of great interest, and there are even two Cynthia poems, though the more detached attitude is maintained. In 4.7, Cynthia is dead, but comes back as ghost to complain to Propertius – and speaks of herself as a topic of his poetry.

The details of Tibullus's life, like those of Propertius, are mostly gathered from his poems, with some references found in Horace and Ovid. Born between 55 and 48 BC (though he may have been a little older than Propertius, given the order of the elegists Ovid lays out in *Tristia* 4.10.53–4), he died young, shortly after Virgil in 19 BC (our evidence for this comes from an epigram of Domitius Marsus; Ovid commemorates his death in *Am.* 3.9). Although he claims *paupertas*, 'poverty', in his poems (e.g. 1.1, but see note on line 5 for the word), he may not, in fact, have been poor. This claim may rather be a conventional elegiac stance of rejecting wealth, or an indication that the reduction of his family fortunes left him *comparatively* poorer, though still of comfortable means (Horace *Epist.* 1.4 depicts him as well-to-do and with a villa at Pedum; if indeed he was of equestrian rank, it suggests comfortable economic standing, as well). Tibullus was not a part of Maecenas's circle, but he was closely associated with M. Valerius Messalla Corvinus, a leading military and political figure as well as the only literary patron to rival Maecenas at the time. In the civil wars, Messalla fought with Brutus and Cassius against Octavian at Philippi, then with Antony, and finally with Octavian at Actium against Antony. He shared the consulship of 31 BC with Octavian, and from Actium onwards served him faithfully. Messalla was made Prefect of Asia Minor and Proconsul of Aquitania, where he suppressed uprisings and was granted a triumph in 27 BC. The occasion is celebrated in Tib. 1.7, and Messalla is also addressed in 1.1, where he, the decorated military hero, is set up as the opposite of the submissive elegiac lover. Although not a part of Maecenas's circle, Tibullus seems to have been friendly with at least one of the poets of this circle, Horace: he addresses an Albius, identified with Tibullus, in two of his poems (*Epist.* 1.4 and *Odes* 1.33).

Of the three books in the so-called *corpus Tibullianum*, only the first two are by Tibullus. The poems in the third book are by various other poets, probably from Messalla's circle; hence the association with Tibullus. Tibullus's first book of 10 elegies deal primarily, like Prop. 1, with the poet's relationship with his mistress, Delia. It does, however, also include love poems addressed to a boy, Marathus (1.4, 8–9), a precedent for which we can find in Catullus's poems to Juventius, which balance his poems for Lesbia. But among the three elegists, Tibullus is the only one to include love poems for a boy. He also stands out for his focus on the countryside instead of the urban setting of Propertius and Ovid. Longing for a quiet life in the country is a central theme in Tibullus, and elements in his pastoral idyll contain echoes of Virgil's *Eclogues* and *Georgics*. Tibullus's first book of elegies was probably published in 27–26 BC given the reference to Messalla's triumph and the collection's apparent influence on Prop. 2. In his second book of elegies both Delia and Marathus are left behind, and there is a new mistress, Nemesis. She seems more stereotyped than Delia, but may also be another side of the same figure. The book contains only six poems, which has led some to think it may have been cut short by Tibullus's death and published posthumously; alternatively, a part of it as we have it may have gone missing.

The prime source for the life of the youngest of the trio, Ovid, as with the other elegists, is his own poetry (esp. *Tristia* 1.2, 4.10). He was born in 43 BC in Sulmo into an established equestrian family and came to Rome to study rhetoric. The elder Seneca (*Controversiae* 2.2.8–12) informs us that Ovid performed in these studies with distinction, and the marks of his education are perceptible in his poetic work, too: his style is often described as 'rhetorical'. He capped his studies with the usual tour of Greece, after which he gave up an administrative career in favour of poetry. By the time Ovid came to Rome, the political unrest of the civil wars was essentially over and the literary scene was thriving. At an early age, Ovid gained the favour of Messalla at public recitations, but despite this association, he was socially and economically secure enough not to need a patron. He was connected to many of the eminent poets of the literary circle and had the privilege of hearing them recite their poetry, though Virgil and Tibullus seem to have died too soon for Ovid to have benefited from their friendship (*Tristia* 4.10.41–52).

Ovid was a prolific writer, and unlike in the case of his fellow elegists, his works extend beyond the genre of love elegy. The *Amores* are love elegies on the model of Propertius and Tibullus (though of course with an Ovidian flavour), featuring Corinna as the poet's mistress and treating different aspects of their relationship. Originally published around 20 BC as five books, a second edition in three books – as they have come down to us – was published around 2 BC (before the *Ars Amatoria*, see below). The *Heroides* continue many of the elegiac themes, though not the same form: they present themselves as letters from mythical heroines to their absent lovers, in some cases with a reply from the man. He composed three didactic poems in elegiacs by 2 AD: *Medicamina Faciei Feminae*, a witty but fragmentary (only 100 lines survive) poem on women's cosmetics; *Ars Amatoria*, 'the Art of Love', where he teaches the art of seduction in the *persona* of *praeceptor amoris*, 'teacher of love' (see below), in the first two books to men, in the last, third book to women; and *Remedia Amoris*, in which he instructs both men and women on how to find a way out of love affairs, a sort of recantation of *Ars Amatoria*. In addition to the subject matter, they depart from the traditional form of didactic poetry of Hesiod and Lucretius, composed in hexameter. Ovid's next work, the *Metamorphoses*, is an epic in hexameter (his only work not in elegiacs) on transformations of men, women and other creatures and things. The narrative is arranged more or less chronologically from the creation of the world to the deification of Julius Caesar after his death (in 44 BC). Ambitious in scope and subject matter, it was the work which Ovid maintains ensures his literary immortality

(*Met.* 15.871–9). At the same time as the *Metamorphoses*, he composed the *Fasti*, an aetiological poem on the events and festivals on the Roman calendar. It, however, was left incomplete (there are only six books of the planned 12, one for each month). Ovid claims (*Tristia* 1.7.13–14) that his *Metamorphoses* were also unfinished when his fortunes changed at the height of his success: in 8 AD, Augustus exiled him to Tomis on the Black Sea. The reasons for the exile remain obscure and disputed, but the irreverence of *Ars Amatoria* is often induced as one possible reason, especially given Augustus's attempts at a moral reform with his marriage legislation. *Tristia* in five books and *Epistulae ex Ponto* in four are elegiac poems addressed from exile to the emperor, to Ovid's third wife who stayed behind in Rome, and other people. Ovid also composed a curse-poem against an unnamed enemy accused of trying to benefit from Ovid's misfortunes; it is entitled *Ibis* and modelled on a poem of the same name by Callimachus. In *Tristia* and *Epistulae ex Ponto* he describes the sufferings of exile and his wretched life in Tomis, and pleads for clemency. But the pleas were to no avail: Ovid died in exile in 17 AD.

The genre and style of the three elegists

Latin love elegy is composed in elegiac couplets, which consist of a hexameter verse followed by a pentameter verse (see below on metre for more). This form combining a hexameter, which is the same metre as that used in heroic epic throughout, and a pentameter, which breaks away from epic, makes elegy simultaneously aware of epic, that other grand genre, and of elegy's *not* being epic itself. This awareness is reflected in the elegists' work, as well, and indeed exploited humorously by Ovid in *Am.* 1.1. The contrast with heroic epic pervades elegy in many ways. The most notable examples of such epic are Homer's *Iliad* and *Odyssey* on the Greek side and Virgil's *Aeneid* on the Roman: long narrative stories told in the third person about heroic characters who excel in battle and survive ordeals and adventures in strange lands. Elegy, however, subverts epic and heroic themes, as well as the form of epic poetry. Besides the metre, love elegies are much shorter poems than the long epics, and they each recount one incident or short episode.

Unlike the third-person narrator of epic, Latin love elegy has a first-person, subjective speaker: it is written as if the poet himself is speaking; the poets even use their own names to refer to themselves (e.g. Prop. 2.14.27, Tib. 1.3.55). It is good to bear in mind, however, that the poems need not be accurately autobiographical, even when they draw on realities of life in first-century BC Rome. Sometimes the fact that they are carefully constructed literary fictions comes through: a poem may seem to be much more articulately and artfully put together than the burst of passion it depicts would allow (e.g. the well thought-out and carefully balanced argumentation of Ovid *Am.* 2.7). Therefore, it is better to think of the 'Propertius', 'Tibullus' and 'Ovid' represented in the poems as the poetic *personae* of each poet, distinct from their actual, historical person. The term *persona* derives from drama, where it means a 'mask' worn by an actor: just as an actor puts on a mask to impersonate a character in a play, so the poet takes up a *persona* in his poems. It may resemble the actual historical person of the poet in some ways, but may have experiences, acquaintances and other traits quite different from those of the real man. The poetic *persona* of the elegist, in fact, has its own conventions: he is a poet *and* a lover, writing poems about and for his mistress. A recurrent aspect of this *persona* is that of a *praeceptor amoris*, 'an instructor of love': having learnt from his own experience, the poet-lover assumes the position of a teacher to educate other lovers (e.g. Prop. 1.1.35–8, 2.14.19–20, Ovid *Am.* 2.5.55–62).

A central element of the genre is the female beloved (with the exception of Tibullus's Marathus) whom the poets celebrate in their elegies. Propertius and Ovid even give the appearance of tracing the development of a relationship from the first falling in love (Prop. 1.1, Ovid *Am.* 1.3) to a disenchanted end (reflected in Prop. 4.7 and Ovid *Am.* 2.19 in our selection). Whether the poems constitute an autobiographical account of a real affair has been disputed, however, since the depiction of the relationship is such a mixture of realistic detail with conventional literary themes that distinguishing fact from fiction becomes difficult. The scant biographical information on the poets does not offer much help in this regard. Apuleius (*Apologia* 10), who provides the identification of Catullus's Lesbia with Clodia, also gives the identity of Propertius's Cynthia as Hostia and of Tibullus's Delia as Plania. The identifications are not entirely convincing, however, and the fact that Apuleius does not offer a historical identity for Ovid's Corinna or Tibullus's Nemesis suggests they are fiction. All the names of the mistresses are, in fact, significant in themselves, including Gallus's Lycoris: Lycorean, Cynthian and Delian are epithets of Apollo, the patron god of poetry. Nemesis means 'Retribution', a suitable name for a difficult elegiac mistress in itself. Catullus's Lesbia evokes the famous love poetess of Lesbos, Sappho, and – probably modelled on Catullus – Ovid's Corinna has the name of another Greek poetess. The mistress thereby is represented as having a privileged connection to poetry, as suits a learned Callimachean reader and recipient of the poet's gift of poems. On the other hand, she can also be seen as the poems' source and inspiration, the poet's personal Muse (e.g. Prop. 2.1.4), and as the subject matter itself (an idea made explicit by Ovid in *Am.* 1.1.19–20, see also Prop. 4.7.50).

The status of the mistress has also occasioned much debate. As a result of the many changes in the first century BC, including social ones, Roman women enjoyed much more freedom than their Greek or Roman predecessors. There were many wealthy, well-educated and politically influential married women, who might take lovers. Clodia, with whom Catullus's Lesbia has been identified, was one example. On the other hand, high-class courtesans and freedwomen would not only be similarly well-educated, but could enjoy the company of influential men, as for example did Cytheris, the mistress of Mark Antony and identified with Gallus's Lycoris. Whatever the actual status of the beloved in our three elegists, it is clear that she enjoys considerable freedom, does not always behave like one might expect a respectable Roman lady to do, and may have other lovers or possibly even a husband (e.g. Prop. 2.14, Tib. 2.4, Ovid *Am.* 2.19).

Whether she is married, a courtesan or something else, however, the aspect of the elegiac relationship that most flew in the face of the social norms was the poet-lover's passionate devotion and submission to his beloved. To a Roman, this would have seemed decadent and a form of slavery. Indeed, the elegiac beloved is regularly called *domina*, 'mistress', the slave's word for his female owner. This is part of the conventional elegiac theme of *servitium amoris*, 'slavery of love'. The poet is at the mercy of his beautiful captor, but willingly so – at least at times, anyway. While some poems celebrate the joys of nights spent with a loving mistress (e.g. Prop. 2.14), many more lament the rejection by the conventionally *dura puella*, 'harsh girl'. One standard scenario is that of an *exclusus amator*, 'a locked-out lover', who complains at his mistress's door and tries in vain to get in (also known as a *paraklausithuron*, '(a song by a locked door'). The mistress can also be fickle and demanding: a common bane of the elegist is a band of richer rivals who win over the mistress with their gifts (Tib. 2.4 combines many of these elements in a complaint about Nemesis's greed). The poet, on the other hand, is conventionally poor: his gift is his poetry, not expensive jewellery.

The poet-lover's slavery to his passions and mistress is contrary to Roman values and the traditional path to distinction through a political or military career, as well. The elegists explicitly reject political and military glory in favour a life of love (Prop. 1.6 sets out an example of the argument). Instead, under the command of their mistresses and Amor, the god of Love, they wage wars of love. Part and parcel with the theme of *militia amoris*, 'the military service of love', are depictions of love-making and lovers' quarrels as battles (e.g. Tib. 1.3.64), the long vigils outside the mistress's door on a par with nightly watches of the soldiers, and the successes of the lover as equal to a triumph celebrating a military victory (e.g. Prop. 2.14.23–4). The opposition of war and love extends to elegy's opposition to epic, as well: just as epic is the genre of war and heroic exploits, so elegy, by being anti-war is also anti-epic.

On the level of style, Callimachus was an important model for the elegists, just as he was for the preceding generations of Roman poets. As a part of the elegists' opposition to war and epic, they employ the *recusatio* on Callimachus's model in a variety of ways (e.g. Prop. 3.3, Ovid *Am.* 1.1). In addition to this *topos*, they make use of vocabulary with literary critical connotations: following the Callimachean ideal, *tenuis*, 'slender', *levis*, 'light' and *tener*, 'delicate', mark their kind of elegant poetry, as opposed to weighty and uncouth epic. Other terms to keep an eye out for are *cultus*, 'cultivated', 'educated', and *doctus*, 'learned', again qualities of this refined poetry, but also those of its expected readership. Urban sophistication is a hallmark of the genre, and in the urbane poetry of Propertius and Ovid this is brought out both literally, in the urban setting and characters of the poem, as well as in its style. For them, the byword for the opposite is *rusticus*, 'rustic', 'country-bumpkin' and therefore 'unsophisticated' (e.g. Ovid *Am.* 2.8.3, where also see note). In Tibullus's poetry with its countryside idyll that word, however, gains positive connotations (e.g. Tib. 1.1.8).

Each of the three elegists of course brings his own characteristics to the genre. In addition to his focus on the countryside, Tibullus's *persona* also stands out as actually serving in the military, thereby adding another layer to the theme of *militia amoris* (1.1 and 1.3

both exemplify this). For him, the country ideal offers a respite from the troubles of contemporary life, such as the corruption of wealth and the city, as well as the hardships of the soldier (e.g. 1.1). Another feature that distinguishes Tibullus among the elegists is his tendency to include several themes within one poem, but transitioning between them smoothly and creating a unified whole out of the multiplicity of strands (e.g. the themes of the country life and love, both contrasted with that of the soldier's lot in Tib. 1.1). In contrast, both Propertius's and Ovid's poems tend to arise from a single occasion or idea.

Propertius, in turn, uses more mythology than Tibullus and Ovid: it is one of his most oft-used resources, and he draws on it in a variety of ways, from extended narrative and mythological *exempla* to allusion and proverb. While some of his poems appear earnestly passionate, he can also bring wry wit and irony to his depiction of love. Ovid, though, perhaps takes this furthest: his playfulness can be detached to the point of being unromantic. Coming at the end of what was by then a fully formed genre, Ovid shows full awareness of its conventions, and often plays with them. For example, he may explore the inconsistencies in the stance of the elegiac lover in a humorously self-mocking way (e.g. the twist at the end of *Am.* 2.5) or demonstrates rhetorical skill in arguing both sides of a case (e.g. *Am.* 2.7 and 2.8).

Summaries of the poems in this selection

These summaries are intended to give an overview of the elegies set for OCR's AS and A-level Latin examination in June 2017–18 and to illustrate the subject matter and features of the genre further. The summaries retain the first-person speaker of the poems themselves, as well as the changes in addressees and quoted direct speech. For further details on the characters and myths referred to in the summaries of the poems set in Latin, see the commentary.

Propertius

1.1 (AS)

Cynthia was the first to capture me, and since then Amor has lorded it over me to the point that I have begun living a dissolute life: this has now lasted a whole year. Tullus, my friend, Milanion's devotion in his pursuit of Atalanta provides a model of successful persistence in love. I am not so lucky, Amor does not help me with cunning plans. But you, witches, make my girl fall in love with me and I will believe in your powers. And you, friends, seek a remedy for an aching heart, however bitter it may be and however far it may take me. You, whom the god favours, stay behind and enjoy your happy love; I, on the other hand, suffer the pangs of love without a break. I advise you to avoid this evil and stay true to your established love – woe to him who heeds my advice too late!

1.3 (A level)

Like the mythical heroines Ariadne and Andromeda, or a Bacchant resting in calm sleep, just so my sleeping Cynthia seemed to me when I came back drunk late at night from a drinking party. Both love and wine pushed me to make an attempt on her, but I did not dare to disturb her sleep for fear of a railing. Instead, I stood and stared at her like Argus at Io. I proceeded to give gifts of love to you, Cynthia, and whenever you sighed, I feared you had an ill-omened dream – until the light of moon woke you up. She propped herself up on the bed and said: 'have you finally come back, after someone else has kicked you out? Where have you spent the night that you should have been with me? I wish you had such nights of suffering! I tried to keep awake by spinning and singing, until sleep overcame me.'

2.14 (A level)

Not so happy was the son of Atreus when Troy fell, nor Odysseus when he reached home after his long wanderings, nor Electra when she saw Orestes safe, or Ariadne when she saw Theseus emerge uninjured from the Labyrinth, as I was when I recalled the joys of the preceding night: another such night will make me immortal! She no longer tries to resist me with unyielding pride. But when I was submissive, I was considered worthless. If only I had learnt the secret sooner! I was blind not to have seen it before. This is what I gathered is more effective: lovers, scorn your beloved! Now others bang at my girl's door – while she is with me. This is my triumph! I will dedicate my spoils to you, Venus, in thanks for the night of love. But now, my darling, our relationship depends on you: if any fault changes your feelings towards me, I will lie dead before your door.

4.7 (A level, in English)

Cynthia appeared to me in my dream as a ghost. She snapped her fingers and said: 'You traitor, you have forgotten about me too quickly, nor did you pay your respects at my funeral. The slave Lygdamus killed me with a potion made by slave Nomas, who has now risen to prominence and wealth at my expense, and she punishes any slave that is complimentary towards me. I do not chide you after all: I did have a long reign in your books. I swear I was faithful to you; for in the underworld, there is a region for adulterous women, including Klytaimnestra who killed her husband Agamemnon and the wife of Minos, Pasiphae, who fell in love with a bull and bore the Minotaur. There is also another region, Elysium, for the faithful lovers, including Andromeda and Hypermnestra. I now give you instructions, in case that other woman Chloris does not entirely have you in her power. Look after my faithful maids well, and burn your poems written in my honour so that you may cease to win praise through me. Plant ivy on my grave and inscribe an epitaph over it. Do not look down on dreams sent from the underworld that have the weight of truth. There are laws that govern the dead: we may roam free at night, but by day must be confined to the underworld. Now other women may have you, but soon you will be mine alone, mixed with my bones in the same grave.' When she was done speaking, her ghost escaped my embrace.

Tibullus

1.1 (AS)

Others may amass wealth through warfare, but let me lead an unwarlike life on my humble means. May I tend my farm myself, and Hope provide me with a harvest, for I worship the gods of the countryside reverently. You, too, Lares of an impoverished estate, accept your gifts: back then, a heifer was sacrificed, now a small lamb. Now, finally, I could live happy with little and not constantly be on long campaigns. I would not be ashamed to work the land and look after the animals. Wolves and thieves, stay away from my flock, for here I worship country gods. I do not need the riches of my forefathers: a small harvest and resting in my own bed is enough. How pleasant it is to hug my mistress when the weather is harsh outside! May this be my lot; may he who can bear the elements be rightly rich. It suits you, Messalla, to wage wars and bring home spoils: I am detained by the chains of a beautiful girl. I do not seek praise, Delia, while I am with you. May I die in your arms. You will mourn for me, because your heart is not of stone. Let us love now, for soon old age will make love unseemly and death will come. It is in the fields of love that I am a good soldier and a commander. May warfare bring riches and wounds to greedy men: with my sufficient store I will look down on the rich and hunger.

1.3 (A level)

You sail away on the Aegean sea without me, Messalla and your cohort, while I am sick and held back on Phaeacia. Death, keep away from me: I do not have anyone to mourn me here, neither mother nor sister – no Delia. Despite omens promising my safe return, she cried and was anxious about my travels; I myself looked for reasons to stay. What use is your Isis to me now, Delia, and your dutiful worship? But, Isis, help me now and Delia will sing your praises. May I worship my ancestral gods at home once again. How happy was life in the Golden Age under Saturn! There was no seafaring for profit, no need for agriculture and domesticating animals, no locked doors, for nature of its own accord provided for all needs of men. There were no wars, but now in the Iron Age under Jupiter, slaughter and dangerous seafaring open up a thousand paths to death. Spare me, father, I have not committed a crime against gods. But if my days are numbered, set a stone with an epitaph on my grave. But, because I have always complied with Amor, Venus herself will guide me to Elysium, where faithful lovers spend their afterlife in games of love. But there is a dark abode of the wicked, where the impious are tormented: may my rivals end up there. But you, Delia, remain faithful. May you spin late into the night, surrounded by your maids: then I will come all of a sudden, then come to me as you are. I pray Aurora may bring this day to pass for us.

2.4 (A level, in English)

I bid farewell to my ancestral freedom: slavery and a mistress await me. I wish I could avoid such suffering – I would rather be a rock exposed to the elements. Now every moment is bitter, and neither elegies nor Apollo, the patron of poetry, help me: my mistress keeps asking for money. I use poetry to gain easy access to a mistress, so leave me alone, Muses, if poems cannot do that. I must now resort to crime to furnish her with gifts and to avoid crying before her locked door. May the merchants of luxury products die! That is what makes girls wicked and keeps doors locked. But at a price, they will open. You who lock out lovers who have been priced out, may your wealth burn and no one help put out the fire. When you die, no one will mourn you. But when a kind and generous girl lives even a hundred years, her death will be mourned and an old lover will bring flowers to her grave. These are true words, but they do not help me. Love must be served in accordance with his own laws. If Nemesis asked me to sell my ancestral home, I would; whatever magic potions she might concoct for me, I would drink, if only she would receive me kindly.

Ovid

1.1 (AS)

I was preparing to write about arms and war in a metre matching the subject matter, but Cupid stole one metrical foot from my verses. 'Who gave you this right over poetry, cruel boy? I belong to the Muses, not you. What mayhem would ensue if gods took over each others' customary roles? You are already powerful enough; why do you ambitiously aspire to new enterprises? I do not have a suitable subject for lighter poetry: no beloved girl or boy.' When I had finished, he at once drew his bow and said, 'receive your task, poet'. Poor me! Now Amor reigns in my empty heart and my poems rise in six and fall in five feet. Farewell, wars with your metre. Put on a myrtle garland, my elegiac Muse.

2.5 (AS)

I wish to die because you have been unfaithful. It is no circumstantial evidence that condemns you; I wish my case were not so good! I myself saw what you did with another man at a dinner party when you thought I was asleep: the secret signs and messages, and when many guests had left, the indecent kisses. 'What are you doing? These are between you and me, and I claim what is rightfully mine.' When I had vented my anger, she blushed in shame. But her blush made her more beautiful than ever: I wanted to attack her but her beauty disarmed me and I begged for kisses instead. She smiled and kissed me all too well – I am pained, since she must have learnt that way of kissing from someone else than me!

2.7 (A level)

Am I to stand accused of new crimes forever? No matter what I do, you accuse me of infidelity. I wish I was guilty! Those who are, bear their punishment calmly. Now your rash allegations undermine your anger; too much scolding makes itself ineffective. Here is the new accusation: that I have slept with your maid Cypassis. May gods grant me better than to take a lowly girlfriend! In addition, why would I pursue a maid so loyal to you, if not to be both rejected and told on? I swear by Venus and Cupid that I did not do it.

2.8 (A level)

Accomplished hairdresser and lover, Cypassis, who told Corinna about us? Surely I gave nothing away. What of it that I claimed no one of sound mind would sleep with a slave-girl? Agamemnon and Achilles loved their slave-girls, and I am no greater than they. When Corinna looked at you, you blushed – but how composed was I when I swore by Venus. For these services, Cypassis, repay me by sleeping with me today. Why do you refuse? If you say no, I will confess all to Corinna.

2.19 (A level, in English)

If you do not need to keep your girl safe for yourself, do it for me: what is allowed holds no charms for me, but the forbidden inspires my passion. I love nothing that causes no pain. Corinna saw this flaw in me, and knew how to ensnare me. Oh, how often she rekindled the fires by exasperating me. What sweet words and kisses she then had in store for me! You, too, who recently caught my eye, often play coy and refuse me, and let me spend cold nights in front of your locked door: that is how my love grows. Whosoever desires what is allowed picks low-hanging fruit. The girl who wants to reign for long must play her lover for a fool – woe me, may my advice not cause me pain! But you, who worry too little about your beautiful girl: begin to lock the door at night and check what messages the maids carry. Be jealous and give my tricks an opportunity. I warn you: if you do not guard her better, she will cease to be mine. I have endured much for long, hoped you would guard her better. You suffer patiently what no husband should – but that will be the end of my love! Oh unhappy me, shall I never be kept away? Shall I not have any vengeance to fear? What do I do with a husband who is a pimp? His complaisance ruins my pleasure. If it pleases you to have me as your rival, say no!

Rhetorical and poetic devices

This glossary illustrates further the stylistic devices employed by the elegists and explains the rhetorical and poetic terms themselves. It is by no means exhaustive; it does not cover all such devices used in the poems, but it includes those mentioned in this book. For more rhetorical devices with English examples and explanations, refer to the 'Silva Rhetoricae' (see further reading).

It should be borne in mind that in the examination, simply identifying the devices does not yield sufficiently probing analysis. The emphasis should be on explaining the effects of the device in its particular context. For example, with the antimetabole below, the intertwined word order of the pronouns (you – me – me – you) emphasizes the intimate sharing between the two, and only the two, to the exclusion of any intruding third party. Further explanation of some of the devices and their effects may be found in the commentary.

Alliteration: repetition of the same sound or letter in nearby words, often the initial consonant.

> quoque loco tecum fuerim quotiensque, Cypassi,
> narrabo dominae quotque quibusque modis. (Ovid *Am.* 2.8.27–8)

Anaphora: repetition of the same word (or group of words) at the beginning of successive clauses.

> haec spolia, haec reges, haec mihi currus erunt. (Prop. 2.14.24)

Antimetabole: repetition of identical words in reversed order (compare chiasmus, from which antimetabole differs in that the words must be identical, if in different forms).

> haec *tibi* sunt mecum, mihi sunt communia *tecum*. (Ovid *Am.* 2.5.31)

Assonance: repetition of the same vowel sounds in nearby words.

> adsiduas atro viscere pascit aves. (Tib. 1.3.76)

Asyndeton: the omission of conjunctions between clauses.

> sex mihi surgat opus numeris, in quinque residat. (Ovid *Am.* 1.1.27)

Chiasmus: repetition of ideas or grammatical structures in reverse order, often illustrated as the ABBA order (contrast antimetabole).

> dites despiciam despiciamque famem. (Tib. 1.1.78)

Ellipsis: omission of a word or phrase easily understood from the context.

an, quod ubique, tuum est? (Ovid *Am*. 1.1.15; *est* omitted in the relative clause)

Epanalepsis: repetition of the same word or clause after intervening matter.

omniaque ingrato largibar **munera** somno,
munera de prono saepe voluta sinu. (Prop. 1.3.25–6)

Epithet: a descriptive adjective or phrase, often a standard one for a given character or object.

rapax Mors (Tib. 1.3.65)

Aoniam ... lyram (Ovid *Am*. 1.1.12)

Hyperbole: rhetorical exaggeration.

cineri nunc medicina datur (Prop. 2.14.16)

Litotes: deliberate understatement, often a double negative.

nec ... littera nulla. (Ovid *Am*. 2.5.18)

Metaphor: a comparison by referring to an object or idea through substituting another for it.

nunc ad te, mea lux, veniatne ad litora navis
servata, an mediis sidat onusta vadis. (Prop. 2.14.29–30)

Metonymy: a comparison by referring to an object or idea through something connected to it. Synecdoche (see below) is a form of metonymy.

illa tua totiens **aera** repulsa manu. (= *sistrum*, Tib. 1.3.24)

furtivae **Veneris** conscia signa dedi? (= love, Ovid *Am*. 2.8.8)

Mythological *exemplum*: an illustration or precedent from myth for comparison or to support a particular point.

> Milanion nullos fugiendo, Tulle, labores
> saevitiam durae contudit Iasidos.
>   …
> ergo velocem potuit domuisse puellam:
> tantum in amore preces et bene facta valent. (Prop. 1.1.9–16)

Onomatopoeia: using a word that imitates the sound of the thing it specifies.

> … serpentum Cerberus ore
> **stridet.** (Tib. 1.3.71–2)

Personification: attributing to inanimate objects the qualities, intentions or actions of humans.

> donec diversas praecurrens luna fenestras,
> luna moraturis sedula luminibus,
> compositos levibus radiis patefecit ocellos. (Prop. 1.3.31–3)

Polyptoton: repetition of a word in a different form.

> has pono ante **tuas tibi**, diva, Propertius aedis. (Prop. 2.14.27)

Recusatio: a formal refusal to compose on a given topic or in a given genre (often not to be taken entirely seriously). The whole of Ovid *Am.* 1.1 is such a rhetorical exercise.

Rhetorical question: a question that does not expect an answer, but rather conveys or implies its unstated conclusion through the question form.

> quid si praeripiat flavae Venus arma Minervae,
> ventilet accensas flava Minerva faces? (Ovid *Am.* 1.1.7–8)

Ring-composition: returning to the themes or vocabulary of the opening of a work at its end.

Divitias alius fulvo sibi congerat auro

...

dites despiciam despiciamque famem. (Tib. 1.1.1, 78)

Sententia: a short, pithy statement, like a proverb.

aequo animo poenam, qui meruere, ferunt. (Ovid *Am.* 2.7.12)

Sibilance: alliteration of *s* sounds.

Tisiphoneque impexa feros pro crinibus angues
saevit. (Tib. 1.3.69–70)

Simile: an explicit comparison, using 'like', 'such as' or a similar expression.

Qualis Thesea iacuit cedente carina
languida desertis Cnosia litoribus;

...

talis visa mihi mollem spirare quietem. (Prop. 1.3.1–7)

Syllepsis: the use of a word with two others it modifies or governs, but in different ways, often to a witty effect (a special kind of **zeugma**).

osculaque admota *sumere* et **arma** manu. (Prop. 1.3.16)

Synchysis: confused arrangement of words in a sentence.

o quotiens ingressus iter mihi tristia dixi
offensum in porta signa dedisse pedem! (Tib. 1.3.19–20)

Synecdoche: using a part to indicate the whole (a subcategory of metonymy).

Qualis Thesea iacuit cedente **carina**. (= ship, Prop. 1.3.1)

Transferred epithet or **hypallage**: shifting the application or order of words so that one agrees grammatically with another with which it does not logically go.

ebria cum multo traherem **vestigia** Baccho. (Prop. 1.3.9)

Tricolon: three parallel elements in a sequence.

haec spolia, haec reges, haec mihi currus erunt. (Prop. 2.14.24)

Greek precursors of love elegy

Although love elegy as we find it in Propertius, Tibullus and Ovid was a Roman innovation, many of its elements have precursors in Greek poetry. The Latin poets themselves often acknowledge their Greek models, and the purpose here is to provide some more details regarding them.

The earliest Greek poetry composed in the same form as Latin love elegy, in elegiac couplets (see below on metre), was used for a wide variety of occasions and topics. These ranged from military exhortations to reflections on friendship and love, and could be performed in settings such as the drinking party (*symposium*). One early Greek elegist was Mimnermus (seventh century BC), who was famous for his poems on love. He dedicated a collection of elegies to a flute-girl called Nanno, and the collection was also named after her. Unlike in Latin love elegy, however, it seems that Mimnermus did not celebrate his love for Nanno in the poems, but addressed to her a collection of elegies on a range of topics. Despite this dissimilarity with the Latin elegists, Propertius recognizes in Mimnermus a valuable model for a lover-poet to follow (Prop. 1.9.9–14).

The next significant stage in the development of Greek elegy took place among the Hellenistic poets (dating to around the third century BC and associated with the court of Alexandria). They treated love and mythological material in both shorter and larger-scale elegies, and used the metre in a variety of contexts, from hymns to didactic poetry. Of the Hellenistic poets, Callimachus of Cyrene (third century BC) has pride of place among the avowed models of the Roman elegists; Propertius (e.g. 3.3, 4.1) and Ovid (e.g. *Rem. Am.* 381–2) explicitly name him as a model for love poetry. Callimachus's most influential work among the Roman poets seems to have been his *Aitia*, an elegiac poem on the origins of such things as Greek religious cults and cities. In its prologue, Callimachus responds to his critics, who question him on why he does not compose a 'continuous poem' on the exploits of kings and heroes; he explains that the criteria for judging poetry are not quantity but artistic skill. When he was about to start writing, Apollo told him to fatten the sacrificial lamb as much as possible, but keep his Muse slender, and ordered him to make his way along untrodden paths. These metaphors represent the Callimachean ideal of the elegant, carefully crafted and slender style and the avoidance of commonly treated topics and genres. Another Hellenistic poet named by the Latin elegists is Philitas of Cos (born c. 340 BC). Only fragments of his works survive, but other Hellenistic and Roman writers (including Callimachus) mention him. This demonstrates his great influence, and he was held up as the model of learned, polished, small-scale poetry. Ovid (*Tristia* 1.6.2) mentions Philitas's love for Bittis, his wife or mistress, to whom he apparently wrote elegiac poems. But we have no evidence of their being subjective love elegies, like those of the Latin elegists. They may have been on different topics – like Mimnermus's *Nanno*.

The personal experience of love was also treated in other genres apart from elegy. For example, Greek poets from early writers to Hellenistic poets and beyond used the genre of epigram for it. Epigram shares with elegy the metrical form of the elegiac couplet (though it is not limited to it). The key difference, however, is that originally epigrams were intended as inscriptions on objects such as tombstones. Over time, though, epigrams became to be composed as literary pieces, as well. Besides the amatory themes, fictitious dedications and epitaphs feature among the literary epigrams, and no doubt influenced the Latin elegists' use of the motifs in their own poetry (e.g. Prop. 2.14.27–8, 4.7.85–6, Tib. 1.3.55–6).

Although not an elegist, Sappho (born in the second half of the seventh century BC), the famous poetess from the island of Lesbos, should not go without mention. She composed poetry in lyric metres, including love poems from a subjective stance. She is a central model for Catullus: the name of his beloved, Lesbia, 'woman from Lesbos', alludes to the poetess. Notably, Catullus 51 translates and adapts Sappho fragment 31, in which she describes the suffering of a lover. Ovid, too, mentions Sappho as a model (e.g. *Rem. Am.* 761).

Metre

The elegiac couplet is the basic unit of elegy. It is composed of a dactylic hexameter followed by a pentameter. The hexameter has six feet, the first four of which can be either dactyls (–∪∪, that is, a long syllable followed by two short ones), or a spondee (– –, two long syllables); a long syllable is thought to be equivalent to two short ones, hence the choice between the two. The fifth foot is almost always a dactyl, and the sixth can be a spondee or a trochee (–∪). The pentameter, as the name suggests, has five feet, or to be more precise, twice two and a half feet: the first two feet are either dactyls or spondees; then comes the half foot of one long syllable; and the second half of the line is almost always two dactyls, again followed by a long syllable. Here is a scheme for the elegiac couplet; the pentameter is traditionally indented by contrast to the hexameter (the choice between a long or two short syllables is indicated by ∪∪, the option between long or short final syllable of the hexameter with ×, and the break between feet with |):

–U̲U̲|–U̲U̲|–U̲U̲|–U̲U̲|–UU|–×
–U̲U̲|–U̲U̲|–//–UU|–UU|–

There are a few useful rules in order to tell the length of a given syllable in Latin. First, you should learn the length of the case endings of nouns and adjectives and the personal endings of verbs (e.g. first declension singular nominative ends in a short syllable, e.g. *puellă*, but in the ablative singular, the final syllable is long, *puellā*). Second, diphthongs, i.e. where there are two vowels in the same syllable, always make the syllable long. The Latin diphthongs are *ae*, *au*, *oi* and *eu* (other vowel combinations span syllables, e.g. *ue* in *puellae* is split between two syllables, but the final *ae* is a diphthong: scanned as *pŭ-ēl-lae*). Third, when a vowel is followed by two consonants, the syllable is scanned long. This happens both when the consonants are in the same word (e.g. *tenēn̄s*) and at the end of one word and the beginning of the next (e.g. *tetigīt carae*). There are a few things to bear in mind in this context, though: *h* does not count as a consonant; *i* is sometimes a vowel, but sometimes a consonant, like *y* in English 'yellow' (e.g. *iurgia*: the first *i*, at the start of the word, is a consonant, but the second *i*, after the *g*, is a vowel); *u* after *q* does not make the following vowel a diphthong, even though they are in the same syllable (e.g. *-qŭe*); *x* and *z* count as double consonants; and when there is a vowel before two consonants, the second of which is either *l* or *r*, the syllable can be either long or short, e.g. *lăcrima*, *dŭplex*).

There is also a rule for omitting syllables in scansion, called elision. If a word ends in a vowel or *m* before another word beginning with a vowel or *h* (but **not** consonantal *i*), its last syllable is elided, and so, omitted in scansion (here put in brackets), e.g. *omniaq(ue) ingrato*, *mec(um) habuit*.

A caesura is a word break in the middle of a foot and marked with *//*. In the hexameter, this normally happens after the first syllable of the third foot; this is called the strong caesura (either –//∪∪ if dactyl, or –//– if spondee). Alternatively, a weak caesura may occur after the second syllable of a dactylic third foot (–∪//∪); in this case, it is usually accompanied by a strong caesura in the second and fourth feet. In the pentameter, the caesura falls in the middle of the verse, after the first two and a half feet (as shown in the scheme above). Here is an example from Tibullus 1.1.9–10 with a strong caesura in the hexameter:

   – – |–∪∪| – // – | – – | – ∪∪|– –
   nec Spes | destitu|at, // sed | frugum | semper a|cervos
   – ∪∪ | – – | – // – ∪∪ | – ∪∪| –
   praebeat | et ple|no // pinguia | musta la|cu.

As in the above example, the caesura may coincide with a clear break in sense, as well. The weak caesura is infrequent in the three elegists, with only Tibullus cultivating it. In this example it is accompanied by caesuras in the second and fourth foot (Tib. 1.3.5):

   – ∪∪| – // – |– ∪ // ∪| – // – | – ∪∪|–∪
   abstine|as, // Mors | atra, // pre|cor: // non | hic mihi |mater.

Metre is more than the form into which words are fitted in poetry: it can be used for stylistic effects and to complement meaning. In general, when a verse has mostly spondaic feet, the rhythm is considered to be slow or weighty, whereas dactyls often convey rapidity. Likewise, the caesura can be used to emphasize a significant break in the progress of the verse, whether coinciding with the sense (as in the above examples) or highlighting emotional constraint or rupture, among other uses. Our three elegists tend to treat the elegiac couplet as a self-contained unit, so that there is a break in sense at the end of the pentameter, and the pentameter often restates or elaborates the idea of the hexameter. However, the sense sometimes runs on from one couplet to the next; this is called enjambment. At times enjambment simply occurs in the context of communicating a longer or more complex idea, at others, it can be employed to convey the spilling over of emotion, breathless pace, and so on.

Further reading

A classic work on the genre aimed at A-Level students and undergraduates:
Lyne, R.O.A.M. (1996), *The Latin Love Poets*, with new Preface, Oxford: Clarendon Press.

Generally on the elegists and their context, also offering further points of view:
Griffin, J. (1985), *Latin Poets and Roman Life*, Chapel Hill: University of North Carolina Press.
Miller, P.A. (ed.), (2002), *Latin Erotic Elegy: An anthology and reader*, London and New York: Routledge.
Whitaker, R. (1983), *Myth and Experience in Roman Love Elegy*, Göttingen: Vandenhoeck and Ruprecht.
Williams, G. (1968), *Tradition and Originality in Roman Poetry*, Oxford: Clarendon Press.
Wyke, M. (1989), 'Mistress and Metaphor in Augustan Elegy', *Helios* 16: 25–47.

On particular aspects or poems of the elegists:
Keith, A. (1992), '*Amores* 1.1: Propertius and the Ovidian programme', in C. Deroux (ed.), *Studies in Latin Literature and Roman History* 6, 327–44, Brussels: Latomus.
Lee, G. (1975), '*Otium cum indignitate*: Tibullus 1.1', in T. Woodman and D. West (eds), *Quality and Pleasure in Latin Poetry*, 94–114, Cambridge: Cambridge University Press.
Lyne, R.O.A.M. (1979), '*Servitium Amoris*', *Classical Quarterly* n.s. 29: 117–30.
Murgatroyd, P. (1975), '*Militia Amoris* and the Roman Elegists', *Latomus* 34: 59–79.

Online resources (accessed November 2015):
'Silva Rhetoricae', a guide to rhetorical terms with examples in English: http://rhetoric.byu.edu.
'Theoi Project', a reference guide to Greek mythology: www.theoi.com.

Text

Propertius

1.1

Cynthia prima suis miserum me cepit ocellis,
    contactum nullis ante cupidinibus.
tum mihi constantis deiecit lumina fastus
    et caput impositis pressit Amor pedibus,
donec me docuit castas odisse puellas   5
    improbus, et nullo vivere consilio.
et mihi iam toto furor hic non deficit anno,
    cum tamen adversos cogor habere deos.
Milanion nullos fugiendo, Tulle, labores
    saevitiam durae contudit Iasidos.   10
nam modo Partheniis amens errabat in antris,
    ibat et hirsutas ille videre feras;
ille etiam Hylaei percussus vulnere rami
    saucius Arcadiis rupibus ingemuit.
ergo velocem potuit domuisse puellam: 15
    tantum in amore preces et bene facta valent.
in me tardus Amor non ullas cogitat artes,
    nec meminit notas, ut prius, ire vias.
at vos, deductae quibus est fallacia lunae
    et labor in magicis sacra piare focis,   20
en agedum dominae mentem convertite nostrae,
    et facite illa meo palleat ore magis!
tunc ego crediderim vobis et sidera et amnes
    posse Cytinaeis ducere carminibus.
et vos, qui sero lapsum revocatis, amici,   25
    quaerite non sani pectoris auxilia.
fortiter et ferrum saevos patiemur et ignes,

AS

sit modo libertas quae velit ira loqui.
ferte per extremas gentes et ferte per undas,
   qua non ulla meum femina norit iter.   30
vos remanete, quibus facili deus annuit aure,
   sitis et in tuto semper amore pares.
in me nostra Venus noctes exercet amaras,
   et nullo vacuus tempore defit Amor.
hoc, moneo, vitate malum: sua quemque moretur   35
   cura, neque assueto mutet amore locum.
quod si quis monitis tardas adverterit aures,
   heu referet quanto verba dolore mea!

1.3

qualis Thesea iacuit cedente carina
   languida desertis Cnosia litoribus;
qualis et accubuit primo Cepheia somno
   libera iam duris cotibus Andromede;
nec minus assiduis Edonis fessa choreis   5
   qualis in herboso concidit Apidano:
talis visa mihi mollem spirare quietem
   Cynthia non certis nixa caput manibus,
ebria cum multo traherem vestigia Baccho,
   et quaterent sera nocte facem pueri.   10
hanc ego, nondum etiam sensus deperditus omnes,
   molliter impresso conor adire toro;
ct quamvis duplici correptum ardore iuberent
   hac Amor hac Liber, durus uterque deus,
subiecto leviter positam temptare lacerto   15
   osculaque admota sumere et arma manu,
non tamen ausus eram dominae turbare quietem,
   expertae metuens iurgia saevitiae;
sed sic intentis haerebam fixus ocellis,
   Argus ut ignotis cornibus Inachidos.   20
et modo solvebam nostra de fronte corollas
   ponebamque tuis, Cynthia, temporibus;
et modo gaudebam lapsos formare capillos;
   nunc furtiva cavis poma dabam manibus;
omniaque ingrato largibar munera somno,   25
   munera de prono saepe voluta sinu;
et quotiens raro duxti suspiria motu,
   obstupui vano credulus auspicio,
ne qua tibi insolitos portarent visa timores,
   neve quis invitam cogeret esse suam: 30
donec diversas praecurrens luna fenestras,
   luna moraturis sedula luminibus,
compositos levibus radiis patefecit ocellos.

A Level

sic ait in molli fixa toro cubitum:

'tandem te nostro referens iniuria lecto   35

    alterius clausis expulit e foribus?

namque ubi longa meae consumpsti tempora noctis,

    languidus exactis, ei mihi, sideribus?

o utinam tales perducas, improbe, noctes,

    me miseram quales semper habere iubes!   40

nam modo purpureo fallebam stamine somnum,

    rursus et Orpheae carmine, fessa, lyrae;

interdum leviter mecum deserta querebar

    externo longas saepe in amore moras:

dum me iucundis lapsam sopor impulit alis.   45

    illa fuit lacrimis ultima cura meis.'

2.14

non ita Dardanio gavisus Atrida triumpho est,
    cum caderent magnae Laomedontis opes;
nec sic errore exacto laetatus Ulixes,
    cum tetigit carae litora Dulichiae;
nec sic Electra, salvum cum aspexit Oresten,   5
    cuius falsa tenens fleverat ossa soror;
nec sic incolumem Minois Thesea vidit,
    Daedalium lino cum duce rexit iter;
quanta ego praeterita collegi gaudia nocte:
    immortalis ero, si altera talis erit.   10
nec mihi iam fastus opponere quaerit iniquos,   13
    nec mihi ploranti lenta sedere potest.   14
at dum demissis supplex cervicibus ibam,   11
    dicebar sicco vilior esse lacu.   12
atque utinam non tam sero mihi nota fuisset   15
    condicio! cineri nunc medicina datur.
ante pedes caecis lucebat semita nobis:
    scilicet insano nemo in amore videt.
hoc sensi prodesse magis: contemnite, amantes!
    sic hodie veniet, si qua negavit heri.   20
pulsabant alii frustra dominamque vocabant:
    mecum habuit positum lenta puella caput.
haec mihi devictis potior victoria Parthis,
    haec spolia, haec reges, haec mihi currus erunt.
magna ego dona tua figam, Cytherea, columna,   25
    taleque sub nostro nomine carmen erit:
'has pono ante tuas tibi, diva, Propertius aedes
    exuvias, tota nocte receptus amans'.
nunc ad te, mea lux, veniatne ad litora navis
    servata, an mediis sidat onusta vadis.   30
quod si forte aliqua nobis mutabere culpa,
    vestibulum iaceam mortuus ante tuum!

A Level

Tibullus

1.1

divitias alius fulvo sibi congerat auro
   et teneat culti iugera magna soli,
quem labor adsiduus vicino terreat hoste,
   Martia cui somnos classica pulsa fugent:
me mea paupertas vitae traducat inerti,   5
   dum meus adsiduo luceat igne focus.
ipse seram teneras maturo tempore vites
   rusticus et facili grandia poma manu:
nec Spes destituat, sed frugum semper acervos
   praebeat et pleno pinguia musta lacu.   10
nam veneror, seu stipes habet desertus in agris
   seu vetus in trivio florida serta lapis:
et quodcumque mihi pomum novus educat annus
   libatum agricolam ponitur ante deum.
flava Ceres, tibi sit nostro de rure corona   15
   spicea quae templi pendeat ante fores;
pomosisque ruber custos ponatur in hortis
   terreat ut saeva falce Priapus aves.
vos quoque, felicis quondam, nunc pauperis agri
   custodes, fertis munera vestra, Lares;   20
tunc vitula innumeros lustrabat caesa iuvencos,
   nunc agna exigui est hostia parva soli:
agna cadet vobis, quam circum rustica pubes
   clamet: 'io messes et bona vina date'.
iam modo, iam possim contentus vivere parvo   25
   nec semper longae deditus esse viae,
sed Canis aestivos ortus vitare sub umbra
   arboris ad rivos praetereuntis aquae.
nec tamen interdum pudeat tenuisse bidentem
   aut stimulo tardos increpuisse boves;   30
non agnamve sinu pigeat fetumve capellae

desertum oblita matre referre domum.
at vos exiguo pecori, furesque lupique,
    parcite: de magno est praeda petenda grege.
hic ego pastoremque meum lustrare quot annis   35
    et placidam soleo spargere lacte Palem.
adsitis, divi, neu vos e paupere mensa
    dona nec e puris spernite fictilibus:
fictilia antiquus primum sibi fecit agrestis
    pocula, de facili composuitque luto.   40
non ego divitias patrum fructusque requiro
    quos tulit antiquo condita messis avo:
parva seges satis est, satis est requiescere lecto
    si licet et solito membra levare toro.
quam iuvat immites ventos audire cubantem   45
    et dominam tenero continuisse sinu!
aut, gelidas hibernus aquas cum fuderit Auster,
    securum somnos igne iuvante sequi!
hoc mihi contingat: sit dives iure furorem
    qui maris et tristes ferre potest pluvias.   50
o quantum est auri pereat potiusque smaragdi,
    quam fleat ob nostras ulla puella vias.
te bellare decet terra, Messalla, marique,
    ut domus hostiles praeferat exuvias:
me retinent vinctum formosae vincla puellae,   55
    et sedeo duras ianitor ante fores.
non ego laudari curo, mea Delia; tecum
    dum modo sim, quaeso segnis inersque vocer.
te spectem, suprema mihi cum venerit hora,
    te teneam moriens deficiente manu.   60
flebis et arsuro positum me, Delia, lecto,
    tristibus et lacrimis oscula mixta dabis.
flebis: non tua sunt duro praecordia ferro
    vincta, nec in tenero stat tibi corde silex.
illo non iuvenis poterit de funere quisquam   65
    lumina, non virgo, sicca referre domum.

tu manes ne laede meos, sed parce solutis
  crinibus et teneris, Delia, parce genis.
interea, dum fata sinunt, iungamus amores:
  iam veniet tenebris Mors adoperta caput;   70
iam subrepet iners aetas, nec amare decebit,
  dicere nec cano blanditias capite.
nunc levis est tractanda Venus, dum frangere postes
  non pudet et rixas inseruisse iuvat.
hic ego dux milesque bonus: vos, signa tubaeque,   75
  ite procul, cupidis vulnera ferte viris,
ferte et opes: ego composito securus acervo
  dites despiciam despiciamque famem.

1.3

ibitis Aegeas sine me, Messalla, per undas,
    o utinam memores ipse cohorsque mei!
me tenet ignotis aegrum Phaeacia terris:
    abstineas avidas Mors modo nigra manus.
abstineas, Mors atra, precor: non hic mihi mater   5
    quae legat in maestos ossa perusta sinus;
non soror, Assyrios cineri quae dedat odores
    et fleat effusis ante sepulcra comis;
Delia non usquam, quae me cum mitteret urbe,
    dicitur ante omnes consuluisse deos.   10
illa sacras pueri sortes ter sustulit: illi
    rettulit e trinis omina certa puer.
cuncta dabant reditus: tamen est deterrita nusquam
    quin fleret nostras respiceretque vias.
ipse ego solator, cum iam mandata dedissem,   15
    quaerebam tardas anxius usque moras;
aut ego sum causatus aves aut omina dira
    Saturnive sacram me tenuisse diem.
o quotiens ingressus iter mihi tristia dixi
    offensum in porta signa dedisse pedem!   20
audeat invito ne quis discedere Amore,
    aut sciet egressum se prohibente deo.
quid tua nunc Isis mihi, Delia, quid mihi prosunt
    illa tua totiens aera repulsa manu,
quidve, pie dum sacra colis, pureque lavari   25
    te (memini) et puro secubuisse toro?
nunc, dea, nunc succurre mihi (nam posse mederi
    picta docet templis multa tabella tuis)
ut mea votivas persolvens Delia voces
    ante sacras lino tecta fores sedeat   30
bisque die resoluta comas tibi dicere laudes
    insignis turba debeat in Pharia.
at mihi contingat patrios celebrare Penates

**A
Level**

reddereque antiquo menstrua tura Lari.
quam bene Saturno vivebant rege, priusquam   35
    tellus in longas est patefacta vias!
nondum caeruleas pinus contempserat undas,
    effusum ventis praebueratque sinum,
nec vagus ignotis repetens compendia terris
    presserat externa navita merce ratem.   40
illo non validus subiit iuga tempore taurus,
    non domito frenos ore momordit equus;
non domus ulla fores habuit, non fixus in agris
    qui regeret certis finibus arva lapis;
ipsae mella dabant quercus, ultroque ferebant   45
    obvia securis ubera lactis oves;
non acies, non ira fuit, non bella, nec ensem
    immiti saevus duxerat arte faber.
nunc Iove sub domino caedes et vulnera semper,
    nunc mare, nunc leti mille repente viae.   50
parce, Pater. timidum non me periuria terrent,
    non dicta in sanctos impia verba deos.
quod si fatales iam nunc explevimus annos,
    fac lapis inscriptis stet super ossa notis:
'hic iacet immiti consumptus morte Tibullus,   55
    Messallam terra dum sequiturque mari'.
sed me, quod facilis tenero sum semper Amori,
    ipsa Venus campos ducet in Elysios.
hic choreae cantusque vigent, passimque vagantes
    dulce sonant tenui gutture carmen aves;   60
fert casiam non culta seges, totosque per agros
    floret odoratis terra benigna rosis;
ac iuvenum series teneris immixta puellis
    ludit, et adsidue proelia miscet Amor.
illic est cuicumque rapax Mors venit amanti,   65
    et gerit insigni myrtea serta coma.
at scelerata iacet sedes in nocte profunda
    abdita, quam circum flumina nigra sonant:

**A
Level**

Tisiphoneque impexa feros pro crinibus angues
    saevit et huc illuc impia turba fugit;   70
tum niger in porta serpentum Cerberus ore
    stridet et aeratas excubat ante fores.
illic Iunonem temptare Ixionis ausi
    versantur celeri noxia membra rota,
porrectusque novem Tityos per iugera terrae   75
    adsiduas atro viscere pascit aves.
Tantalus est illic, et circum stagna, sed acrem
    iam iam poturi deserit unda sitim;
et Danai proles, Veneris quod numina laesit,
    in cava Letheas dolia portat aquas.   80
illic sit quicumque meos violavit amores,
    optavit lentas et mihi militias.
at tu, casta, precor, maneas sanctique pudoris
    adsideat custos sedula semper anus.
haec tibi fabellas referat positaque lucerna   85
    deducat plena stamina longa colu,
ac circa gravibus pensis adfixa puella
    paulatim somno fessa remittat opus.
tunc veniam subito, nec quisquam nuntiet ante,
    sed videar caelo missus adesse tibi.   90
tunc mihi, qualis eris longos turbata capillos,
    obvia nudato, Delia, curre pede.
hoc precor, hunc illum nobis Aurora nitentem
    Luciferum roseis candida portet equis.

A
Level

Ovid *Amores*

1.1

arma gravi numero violentaque bella parabam
    edere, materia conveniente modis.
par erat inferior versus; risisse Cupido
    dicitur atque unum surripuisse pedem.
'quis tibi, saeve puer, dedit hoc in carmina iuris?   5
    Pieridum vates, non tua, turba sumus.
quid si praeripiat flavae Venus arma Minervae,
    ventilet accensas flava Minerva faces?
quis probet in silvis Cererem regnare iugosis,
    lege pharetratae virginis arva coli?   10
crinibus insignem quis acuta cuspide Phoebum
    instruat, Aoniam Marte movente lyram?
sunt tibi magna, puer, nimiumque potentia regna:
    cur opus adfectas ambitiose novum?
an, quod ubique, tuum est? tua sunt Heliconia tempe?   15
    vix etiam Phoebo iam lyra tuta sua est?
cum bene surrexit versu nova pagina primo,
    attenuat nervos proximus ille meos.
nec mihi materia est numeris levioribus apta,
    aut puer aut longas compta puella comas.'   20
questus eram, pharetra cum protinus ille soluta
    legit in exitium spicula facta meum
lunavitque genu sinuosum fortiter arcum
    'quod' que 'canas, vates, accipe' dixit 'opus'.
me miserum! certas habuit puer ille sagittas: 25
    uror, et in vacuo pectore regnat Amor.
sex mihi surgat opus numeris, in quinque residat;
    ferrea cum vestris bella valete modis.
cingere litorea flaventia tempora myrto,
    Musa per undenos emodulanda pedes.   30

2.5

nullus amor tanti est (abeas pharetrate Cupido),
    ut mihi sint totiens maxima vota mori.
vota mori mea sunt, cum te peccasse recordor,
    in mihi perpetuum nata puella malum.
non mihi deceptae nudant tua facta tabellae   5
    nec data furtive munera crimen habent.
o utinam arguerem sic, ut non vincere possem!
    me miserum, quare tam bona causa mea est?
felix, qui quod amat defendere fortiter audet,
    cui sua 'non feci' dicere amica potest.   10
ferreus est nimiumque suo favet ille dolori,
    cui petitur victa palma cruenta rea.
ipse miser vidi, cum me dormire putares,
    sobrius apposito crimina vestra mero:
multa supercilio vidi vibrante loquentes;   15
    nutibus in vestris pars bona vocis erat.
non oculi tacuere tui conscriptaque vino
    mensa, nec in digitis littera nulla fuit.
sermonem agnovi, quod non videatur, agentem
    verbaque pro certis iussa valere notis.   20
iamque frequens ierat mensa conviva relicta;
    compositi iuvenes unus et alter erant:
inproba tum vero iungentes oscula vidi
    (illa mihi lingua nexa fuisse liquet),
qualia non fratri tulerit germana severo,   25
    sed tulerit cupido mollis amica viro;
qualia credibile est non Phoebo ferre Dianam,
    sed Venerem Marti saepe tulisse suo.
'quid facis?' exclamo 'quo nunc mea gaudia defers?
    iniciam dominas in mea iura manus.   30
haec tibi sunt mecum, mihi sunt communia tecum:
    in bona cur quisquam tertius ista venit?'
haec ego, quaeque dolor linguae dictavit; at illi

conscia purpureus venit in ora pudor.
quale coloratum Tithoni coniuge caelum   35
    subrubet, aut sponso visa puella novo;
quale rosae fulgent inter sua lilia mixtae
    aut, ubi cantatis, Luna, laborat equis;
aut quod, ne longis flavescere possit ab annis,
    Maeonis Assyrium femina tinxit ebur: 40
his erat aut alicui color ille simillimus horum,
    et numquam casu pulchrior illa fuit.
spectabat terram: terram spectare decebat;
    maesta erat in vultu: maesta decenter erat.
sicut erant (et erant culti) laniare capillos   45
    et fuit in teneras impetus ire genas;
ut faciem vidi, fortes cecidere lacerti:
    defensa est armis nostra puella suis.
qui modo saevus eram, supplex ultroque rogavi
    oscula ne nobis deteriora daret.   50
risit et ex animo dedit optima, qualia possent
    excutere irato tela trisulca Iovi:
torqueor infelix, ne tam bona senserit alter,
    et volo non ex hac illa fuisse nota.
haec quoque quam docui multo meliora fuerunt,   55
    et quiddam visa est addidicisse novi.
quod nimium placuere, malum est, quod tota labellis
    lingua tua est nostris, nostra recepta tuis.
nec tamen hoc unum doleo, non oscula tantum
    iuncta queror, quamvis haec quoque iuncta queror: 60
illa nisi in lecto nusquam potuere doceri;
    nescioquis pretium grande magister habet.

AS

2.7

ergo sufficiam reus in nova crimina semper?
   ut vincam, totiens dimicuisse piget.
sive ego marmorei respexi summa theatri,
   elegis e multis unde dolere velis;
candida seu tacito vidit me femina vultu,   5
   in vultu tacitas arguis esse notas;
si quam laudavi, miseros petis ungue capillos,
   si culpo, crimen dissimulare putas;
sive bonus color est, in te quoque frigidus esse,
   seu malus, alterius dicor amore mori.   10
atque ego peccati vellem mihi conscius essem:
   aequo animo poenam, qui meruere, ferunt.
nunc temere insimulas credendoque omnia frustra
   ipsa vetas iram pondus habere tuam:
aspice, ut auritus miserandae sortis asellus   15
   adsiduo domitus verbere lentus eat.
ecce, novum crimen: sollers ornare Cypassis
   obicitur dominae contemerasse torum.
di melius, quam me, si sit peccasse libido,
   sordida contemptae sortis amica iuvet!   20
quis Veneris famulae conubia liber inire
   tergaque conplecti verbere secta velit?
adde quod ornandis illa est operosa capillis
   et tibi per doctas grata ministra manus:
scilicet ancillam quae tam tibi fida, rogarem?   25
   quid, nisi ut indicio iuncta repulsa foret?
per Venerem iuro puerique volatilis arcus
   me non admissi criminis esse reum.

A
Level

2.8

ponendis in mille modos perfecta capillis,
  comere sed solas digna, Cypassi, deas,
et mihi iucundo non rustica cognita furto,
  apta quidem dominae sed magis apta mihi,
quis fuit inter nos sociati corporis index?   5
  sensit concubitus unde Corinna tuos?
num tamen erubui? num verbo lapsus in ullo
  furtivae Veneris conscia signa dedi?
quid quod in ancilla si quis delinquere possit,
  illum ego contendi mente carere bona?   10
Thessalus ancillae facie Briseidos arsit,
  serva Mycenaeo Phoebas amata duci:
nec sum ego Tantalide maior nec maior Achille;
  quod decuit reges, cur mihi turpe putem?
ut tamen iratos in te defixit ocellos,   15
  vidi te totis erubuisse genis.
at quanto, si forte refers, praesentior ipse
  per Veneris feci numina magna fidem!
(tu, dea, tu iubeas animi periuria puri
  Carpathium tepidos per mare ferre Notos.)   20
pro quibus officiis pretium mihi dulce repende
  concubitus hodie, fusca Cypassi, tuos.
quid renuis fingisque novos, ingrata, timores?
  unum est e dominis emeruisse satis.
quod si stulta negas, index ante acta fatebor   25
  et veniam culpae proditor ipse meae,
quoque loco tecum fuerim quotiensque, Cypassi,
  narrabo dominae quotque quibusque modis.

Commentary Notes

Propertius

1.1

The first poem of the book occupies a significant place in the collection. It is where an author traditionally unfolds his poetic programme: his subject matter, tone, style and genre, and he may indicate his place in the literary tradition. This poem, therefore, serves as an excellent introduction to Propertius's collection of poems. The very first word tells us his topic: Cynthia, his beloved; and the adjective describing the poet-lover himself in the same line, *miserum*, 'pitiable' already gives us the tone of the relationship. The love he writes about is a very passionate but unhappy one: Cynthia does not reciprocate his feelings.

The poem opens with an explanation of Propertius's current, unhappy situation and how he came to be a love elegist (1–8). He then turns to address Tullus (9), the nephew of L. Volcatius Tullus, consul in 33 BC with Octavian, and, in addition to this poem, the addressee of 1.6, 14 and 22. Addressing the first poem of the collection to Tullus constitutes a dedication of the book to him. The address to Tullus begins the myth of Milanion and Atalanta used as a point of comparison for Propertius's own situation (9–18). In the rest of the poem Propertius addresses further groups of people: first he asks witches for help (19–24), then his friends (25–30). Finally, he commends happy lovers and contrasts their fortune with his (31–4) and closes the poem with advice – and a warning – to lovers (35–8).

1 Cynthia – emphatically placing the name of his mistress first, Propertius gives us the subject of his poems, or their Muse. Cynthia dominates from the start. **Cynthia prima** . . . **me cepit**, literally, 'Cynthia first captured me', but perhaps in more natural English 'Cynthia was the first to capture me'. *prima* here, in addition to its adverbial meaning 'first', may carry a hint of 'excellent, rare'. In another poem, 3.15, Propertius tells us that there has been another woman, Lycinna – how literally should we take him here? **suis** . . . **ocellis**, the means of capture surrounds its object, *me miserum*, visually illustrating the poet's captivity.

2 contactum – this describes *me miserum* in the previous line further. It blends the associations of two of its meanings, 'hit' (by an arrow) and 'infected' (with a disease).

3 mihi constantis deiecit lumina fastus – *mihi* is dative of disadvantage, but it is translated most naturally as a possessive 'my' modifying *lumina*, a common poetic expression for 'eyes', though here perhaps better 'look'. *constantis* . . . *fastus* are genitive, 'of steadfast pride', and describe *lumina*: 'my look of steadfast pride'. Although *constans* has morally positive connotations, *fastus* is usually a kind of arrogant independence of which Romans disapproved – and so does Propertius elsewhere in his poems (3.12.9–10).

5 castas odisse puellas – there is much debate as to how these words should be interpreted. While some take 'to hate' to be too strong a meaning for *odisse* here, it is suitably dramatic and fits the emotional intent. Furthermore, there is irony in Love as the teacher of hating, and the paradox conveys just how upside down Propertius's world has turned. This is continued in the object of his hate: a proper Roman could be expected to respect, if not love, *castas puellas*. *casta* refers generally to someone above reproach, untouched by scandal. In the context of love elegy it can refer specifically to a mistress faithful to one lover. 'Respectable' could work as a translation here. There has been much debate over the specific reference of *castas puellas* and whether Cynthia is one of them. Suggestions range from respectable Roman ladies in general to women who reject their lover's wooing and even to the nine Muses, patron goddesses of poetry. Decisive consensus over the issues has not been reached, and perhaps Propertius is intentionally ambiguous here.

6 improbus – describes Amor two lines earlier: Propertius is deflecting the term that could well be used of someone who hates *castas puellas* from himself to Amor. **nullo vivere consilio** presents us with another thing Amor has taught Propertius to do. *consilium* refers to rational and practical sense that helps people to achieve their purpose, and Propertius is to live with none of this.

7 toto . . . anno – ablative of 'time within which' is used commonly in poetry instead of accusative of duration: 'for a whole year'. **furor** refers to an intense kind of madness, and is commonly used by ancient authors to describe (destructive) love. The word order elegantly reflects the situation depicted: as *furor* occupies the space between *toto* and *anno* on the page, so it occupies Propertius's entire year.

8 adversos cogor habere deos – as in the previous line, the word order plays out Propertius's being surrounded by hostile gods.

9–16 – these verses present a mythological *exemplum* to illustrate Propertius's situation through a comparison with a mythical hero. Milanion was the successful suitor of Atalanta, the daughter of Iasus. She was a famously fast runner (as is indicated also here with *velocem . . . puellam* in 15), and challenged her suitors to a foot race for her hand. According to the myth, Milanion won the race by dropping three golden apples, which Atalanta stopped to pick up, but interestingly, Propertius focuses on other details instead.

9 Tulle – vocative of Tullus (see introduction to the poem). From the other poems addressed to him, Tullus emerges as a respectable Roman pursuing the expected laudable career path of military service and public honours. He serves as a contrast to the elegiac lover who is concerned with his own private love affair and prefers victories in it to the glories of military feats. He also comes across as a generous and supportive friend of Propertius – and so is an appropriate addressee here. **labores**, 'toils', suggests heroic labours such as those of Hercules, and so raises Milanion's feats to a grand, heroic status.

10 saevitiam durae contudit Iasidos – *saevitia* is a word often used in elegy for the harshness of the mistress when she spurns the lover's approaches, and *dura* is her standard epithet in this context. *Iasidos* is the genitive of the Greek patronymic, 'of the daughter of Iasus', a learned touch.

11 Partheniis amens errabat in antris – Mount Parthenius is in Arcadia, the home of Atalanta and Milanion, and where Iasus was king. Although *antrum* usually means 'cave', 'grotto' or a space protected by an overhanging rock, it can also refer to a (rocky) glen or valley: *Partheniis . . . in antris* = 'in Parthenian glens'. *amens* shows Milanion in the grips of madness, like Propertius (*furor*, 7), and plays on the pun with *amans*, 'loving', 'lover'.

12 ibat et . . . videre – *videre* is an infinitive expressing purpose after *ibat*; *et* is transposed poetically after *ibat*, but should be translated before it, 'and he went to see'. Although the *exemplum* begins with Milanion's *labores*, here we see him simply *looking at* wild beasts: his heroism is humorously undermined.

13 Hylaei percussus vulnere rami – Hylaeus was a Centaur who tried to rape Atalanta but, according to some, was killed by her. Propertius pictures Milanion as present and defending her – and suffering for her sake to demonstrate the dedication of the elegiac lover. The contorted syntax reflects the highly-wrought style of the passage, literally 'struck (*percussus*) by a wound (*vulnere*) of the branch of Hylaeus (*Hylaei . . . rami*)'. *rami* is usually taken to be metonymical for the Centaur's weapon: naturally, it could be a 'club' (made from a branch), but comparison with other versions of the myth suggest 'bow' (also made from a branch). Either way, 'wound from the club/bow' gives the most natural English.

15 domuisse – the perfect infinitive is used, as often in elegiac poetry, synonymously with the present infinitive: 'he was able to tame'.

17 in me tardus Amor . . . cogitat artes – seems to blend meanings of *cogitare in* 'be disposed towards' and *cogitare artes* 'think up crafts, stratagems'. *tardus*, in addition to 'slow (in coming to help)', can also mean 'unpropitious' – as with *cogitare*, the meanings are blended here. The result is that Amor is simultaneously unpropitiously disposed towards Propertius and slow in coming to his help with stratagems in love. *tardus* and *artes* also recall aspects of the story of Milanion and Atalanta that are left implicit here: the first points to a contrast with the swiftness of the girl, and the second alludes to the trick of the golden apples Milanion used to win her. Neither speed nor trickery is available to Propertius.

19 quibus – dative of possession with *est*, 'who have', though in more natural English 'who know the trick...'. Those who can draw the moon down from the heavens are witches (further reinforced in 24 by *Cytinaeis*, 'of Cytina', a town in Thessaly, which was famous for witches). **deductae ... lunae** are in the genitive, 'the trick of the drawn-down moon', but changing the passive construction to an active one results in better English, 'of drawing down the moon'. The phrase also is a way of referring to an eclipse of the moon, in which its brightness fades.

20 labor – also constructed with *quibus* in the previous line, but a different translation gives more natural sense: 'whose work'. **sacra piare** usually means 'to appease (an offended god)' or 'expiate (a religious offence)', meanings which have troubled commentators in a context with witches and magic. **in magicis ... focis**, 'at magical hearths', gives these expiating rites an appropriate tone, however: the gods for whom the rites are performed are underworld gods, perhaps even the spirits of the deceased. They would respond to magic and could provide support in further magic.

21 en agedum ... convertite – *en* is an interjection to catch the witches' attention; *agedum* is a strengthening word emphasizing the imperative *convertite*, 'look, come then and change'. **dominae** signals the theme of *servitium amoris*, the slavery of love.

22 meo ... ore – dative of comparison after *magis*, 'than my face'. **palleat** suggest not merely literal paleness but the traditional symptom of love-sickness: Propertius wants Cynthia to feel as he does now.

23 tunc ego crediderim – 'then I would believe' (i.e. if you witches can perform the demanding trick of changing my girl's mind). The construction that follows, ***vobis ... / posse ... ducere***, combines *credo* with dative ('believe, have faith in' someone) and *credo* with accusative object ('believe that'): *credo* with both accusative and dative can mean 'believe someone (dative) when he says something (accusative)'. We may, therefore, render the phrase with 'I would believe your claim to be able to...' or 'I would believe you can ...'.

24 ducere – this picks up *deductae* from 19, 'divert the stars and rivers (from their natural path)'.

25 sero – opinion is divided as to whether this goes with *lapsum*, 'one who has fallen late' (implying Propertius has resisted love for a long time and only recently fallen victim to it), or *revocatis*, 'you call back too late'. The latter is perhaps more attractive given the overall tone of helplessness in love – a suggestion of a pessimistic prognosis for Propertius's chances of being cured.

AS

26 non – goes with *sani* (it is not a delayed negation of *quaerite*), 'not well', 'sick'. This firmly returns us to the theme of love as a disease begun in 2.

27 ferrum . . . ignes – stand metonymically for the proposed cures from the madness of love, surgery and cautery. But they would equally well apply to torture to which slaves might be subjected, and so suggest the theme of *servitium amoris*. *ignes* themselves are frequently used as a metaphor for love and its passions, and **saevos**, which qualify them, brings us back to the theme of the *saevitia* of the mistress.

28 libertas quae velit ira loqui – the antecedent of *quae* is suppressed, 'those things which'. *loqui* goes with *libertas*: 'freedom to say those things which my rage wants (to say)'.

30 qua – 'where'. **norit** is a contracted form of *noverit*: the perfect subjunctive expresses a wish, 'may know'.

31 facili . . . annuit aure – combines the ideas of a god hearing the lovers' prayers readily (*facili aure*, 'with an easy, favourable, ear') and assenting to their requests (*annuit*, 'nodded'). Here Propertius seems to address yet another group; this time, however, he is not asking for help, but recommending their happy state.

33 in me – 'in my case' or 'against me'; either way, a contrast with *vos* in 31, and an echo of *in me* in 17. **Venus noctes exercet** metaphorically depicts the goddess as training the lover like an athlete through sleepless nights. This could stand for the lover's hoped-for love-making night after night, but **amaras** left at the very end of the verse reveals these as nights of suffering from unrequited love. There may also be a pun on *amaras* and *amoris*, as the expected nights of love turn out to be bitter instead. Therefore, 'harries' or 'torments' can be used to render *exercet* into English here.

AS

34 vacuus . . . Amor – *vacuus* spells out the lover's suffering in the previous line: his is an idle, ineffectual love.

35–6 sua quemque moretur / cura – *cura*, 'care', 'object of concern' can also mean the object of one's love, 'sweetheart'. *moretur* is optative subjunctive, expressing a wish for the ideal state of the lover, literally 'may his own mistress detain each one'. However, more natural English may be achieved by making 'each' the subject: 'may each (lover) stay with his own mistress'.

36 assueto . . . amore – ablative absolute with a temporal sense, 'when the love has become familiar'.

37 quod si quis – 'but if anyone'. **tardas** recalls the unhelpfulness of Amor in 17, and the echo is apt: just as Amor has been of no help to Propertius, the poet's advice is equally useless to those who heed his advice too late. In advising, Propertius takes on the role of *praeceptor amoris*, an instructor of love, recurrent in elegy.

AS

1.3

In this poem we find Propertius in a relationship with Cynthia, though not without troubles. He has been at a drinking party, and comes, still drunk, to Cynthia late at night. She has been waiting for him, but by now she has fallen asleep; at the end of the poem she wakes up and rebukes Propertius. The poem offers elegant examples of Propertius's exploitation of the *topoi* of the genre, from *militia amoris* (12–16) and *servitium amoris* for the harsh mistress (17–18) to the complaint of the locked-out lover (35–40), as well as his use of myth. It does all this with a skilful mixture of humour and passionate sentiment, all befitting an inebriated and besotted lover-poet.

The poem progresses from third-person description of Cynthia (1–20) via second-person address by Propertius to her (21–33) to her own first-person speech (34–46). It opens with three similes illustrating the sleeping Cynthia (1–10). The poet then describes his impulsive attraction to her, yet refraining from laying a finger on her (11–20), opting instead to fawn on her with gifts until she is woken up by the moonlight (21–33). The poem culminates in presenting us with a very different Cynthia from the one Propertius imagines while she sleeps: the calm, restful beauty is replaced by a sharp and querulous mistress rebuking her wayward lover (34–46).

1 Thesea – this adjective, derived from the proper name Theseus, describes **carina**. They form an ablative absolute with **cedente**, 'when the ship of Theseus was receding'. *carina*, literally 'keel', is an example of synecdoche.

2 languida . . . Cnosia – *languida* is somewhat ambiguous: it can be simply 'languid, limp' of someone worn out by travel and anguish of being abandoned, like Ariadne, or it can have the meaning – as it does at 37 – of one relaxed in post-coital exhaustion. This is the first of several of the poem's ambivalent adjectives, at first appearing to have one straightforward meaning, but gaining more from a second instance later on. As with *Thesea*, *Cnosia* is an adjective formed from a name, Cnossos, and means 'the Cnosian (girl)', i.e. Ariadne. After helping Theseus kill the Minotaur, the Cretan princess Ariadne sailed with Theseus as he returned to Athens. Theseus, however, left her behind on the island of Naxos because Dionysus caused him to forget about her: the god was himself in love with Ariadne. The use of adjectives formed from names such as *Thesea* and *Cnosia* (and below, *Cepheia* and *Edonis*) is a learned, Callimachean touch.

3 qualis et – the word order is reversed: *et* should be taken first. **Cepheia** is formed from a proper name, Cepheus, king of Ethiopia, and means 'daughter of Cepheus', Andromeda. She was chained to a rock as a sacrifice to a sea monster, but saved from her doom by Perseus. **accubuit** normally refers to one reclining at table, but in Propertius it almost always has an erotic significance, 'sleep with'. With no partner mentioned for Andromeda (or Cynthia), the latter meaning is not explicit here, however, though a suggestion of it may remain, so we should render it simply as 'was lying down'.

5 Edonis – literally, 'an Edonian woman'. The Edoni were a people of Thrace, and this form is often used to signify a Bacchant, as here. Bacchants were followers of Dionysus and their rituals were distinguished by revelry and dancing.

6 in herboso ... Apidano – Apidanus is a river in Thessaly. *in* + ablative can mean either 'beside', 'on the (grassy) banks of' or simply 'in'; in the latter case, what would be imagined is the dried up grassy river-bed of Apidanus, not an unusual picture in a warmer and drier climate, such as that of Italy.

7 talis – we finally see the object of comparison, Cynthia. **mollem spirare quietem**, 'breathing a gentle rest', is a pointed image, suggesting the volatility of Cynthia's sleep (furthered by *non certis . . . manibus* in the following line). *spirare* is more commonly used of strong emotions, such as rage, and combining it here with *mollem quietem* produces tension and anticipation of what would happen if she woke up.

7–8 visa mihi . . . / Cynthia – with *est* suppressed, 'Cynthia seemed to me'. *visa* also suggests awareness of the distinction between the real and the apparent: Propertius, looking back after the moment in the poem, can reflect on how his later experience corrects his initial impression.

8 nixa – the deponent perfect participle describes Cynthia as 'leaning', 'resting' her head. *nitor* takes the ablative of the thing leant on, here **non certis . . . manibus**: Cynthia's hands are not a steady pillow for her head.

9 ebria cum multo traherem vestigia Baccho – *ebria* describes *vestigia*: the poet's drunkenness is transferred from him to his footsteps (a transferred epithet). *multo . . . Baccho* is an example of metonymy: the name of the god is used to signify one of his gifts, wine ('with much wine'), though a hint of divine inspiration is not inappropriate here, either. The convoluted word order of the verse illustrates the meaning neatly: it is as zigzaggy as you would expect the drunken poet's path to be.

10 sera nocte – ablative of 'time when': 'late at night'. **pueri** refers to the slaves accompanying the poet through the dark streets; that they need to shake the torches to keep them lit indicates just how late it is. *pueri* can also have a metaphorical meaning of 'Cupids'; the torch, likewise, is a metaphor for the flame of love which they fan and incite. Both meanings can be relevant here.

11 nondum etiam – is essentially the same as simple *nondum*, 'not yet'. **sensus omnes** is accusative of respect with the perfect passive participle

A
Level

deperditus, 'destroyed as to all my senses'. However, translating it as active gives the most natural English, 'having lost all my senses'.

12 molliter impresso conor adire toro – *impresso toro* is an ablative absolute and can be rendered by making it active and keeping *ego* as subject, 'having leant on the bed, I try'. Some commentators like to take it to describe Cynthia's sinking into the bed, however, and the Latin is flexible enough to allow either meaning. *adire* means 'reach', 'approach', but the approach can have a sexual meaning. *molliter*, 'gently', can modify either *impresso toro* or *adire*, and emphasizes Propertius's care in not disturbing his mistress's sleep, or the gentle lightness of Cynthia if we take *impresso toro* to indicate how she lies on the bed.

13 duplici correptum ardore – *correptum* refers to the poet, whom the gods Amor and Bacchus command (*iuberent*, subjunctive in the concessive clause, 'although they commanded me'). *duplici ardore* is ablative of means, 'seized by a double passion'. *ardor*, literally 'fire', is used metaphorically for the lover's passion.

14 hac Amor hac Liber – Liber is an Italian god of vegetation identified with the Greek Bacchus, and recalls the metonymical sense at 9. *hac* is adverbial ablative, 'Amor this way and Bacchus that way'. Propertius's double passion is inspired by the two gods and what they represent, love and wine.

15 subiecto leviter positam temptare lacerto – as with molliter in 12, the use of *leviter* is ambiguous: it describes either Propertius's actions (the ablative absolute *subiecto . . . lacerto* or *temptare*, 'to put my arm under and make an attempt lightly'), or Cynthia (*positam*, 'lightly lying'). The ambiguity may be intentional, so the lightness is dispersed throughout the line. Propertius makes the contemplated assault on his mistress a scheme of the gods imposed on him by their order: the basic meaning of *temptare* is 'touch, feel'; its military sense of 'attack,

A Level

assail' is perhaps also suggested here, along with an allusion to the theme of *militia amoris*.

16 osculaque . . . sumere et arma – *sumere* has both *oscula* and *arma* as its objects in a syllepsis, with a metaphorical meaning for *arma sumere*, 'to take up arms', in the sense of beginning the act of love (in contrast to a literal meaning for *oscula sumere*, 'to snatch kisses'). This continues the theme of *militia amoris*.

17 ausus eram – the pluperfect tense emphasizes the ineffectuality of the gods' command – the poet is more in awe of his mistress – but can be rendered with the expected past tense, 'I did not dare'. Indeed, referring to Cynthia with **dominae** here indicates a shift to the theme of *servitium amoris* and the lover's submission to his mistress.

18 expertae metuens iurgia saevitiae – *expertae saevitiae* (literally, 'of the cruelty that had been experienced': the perfect participle of the deponent *experior* has a passive meaning) shows us that Propertius has experienced his mistress's cruelty before, and now, based on that experience, is afraid of causing an altercation, 'fearing a railing from the cruelty I had experienced before'.

19 intentis haerebam fixus ocellis – Propertius is triply halted: 'transfixed (*fixus*) with my eyes strained (*intentis ocellis*), I was standing still (*haerebam*, literally 'I was clinging')'.

20 Argus ut ignotis cornibus Inachidos – *ut* should be translated first and begins a simile. Argus was a hundred-eyed monster set by jealous Juno to guard Io, one of Jupiter's loves and the daughter of Inachus (hence *Inachidos*, a genitive of the Greek patronymic, 'of the daughter of Inachus'). To hide his affair from Juno, Jupiter turned Io into a cow. Juno was suspicious, however, and demanded the cow for herself, a request Jupiter could not refuse. She then set Argus as Io's guardian. Describing the horns (*cornibus*) of Io as *ignotis*, 'unfamiliar' or 'strange', suggests wonder as well as something frightening.

A Level

21–6 – the imperfect tenses and repeated words (*et modo solvebam . . .
/ ponebamque . . . / et modo gaudebam . . . / . . . dabam . . . / . . . munera
. . . / munera*) in these lines reflect the continued and repeated actions
of Propertius in his attempts to give his sleeping mistress gifts. The
anaphora of *et modo* (21–3) and the epanalepsis of *munera* (25–6)
supply emphasis to Propertius's solicitousness towards his mistress as
well as illustrating his drunkenness.

21 corollas – 'garlands', would be worn by participants at a drinking
party such as the one from which Propertius is returning, but they are
also suitable gifts from a lover to his beloved.

22 tuis, Cynthia, temporibus – here the poet turns to address his
mistress directly, 'onto your temples, Cynthia'. The shift from describing
her in the third person to a second person address is a step towards a
more immediate interaction between her and Propertius – and a
more vivid and real Cynthia for the audience.

24 poma – 'apples', like the garlands, are gifts which Propertius could
have brought from the drinking party, but (more significantly) they
are the love gift *par excellence*. **cavis manibus** could be the dative of
the hands receiving the gifts, but since Cynthia is using hers as her
pillow (8), it is more likely the ablative of means for Propertius's hands.
cavis means that they are cupped in a protective gesture to enclose the
apples: 'with cupped hands'.

25 – the expression of the lover's generosity – and the ingratitude of
the recipient – reach a hyperbole here. **omniaque munera**, 'and all
(my) gifts' are juxtaposed (even intertwined in the word order) with
ingrato somno, 'to ungrateful sleep'. **largibar** further indicates lavish
gift-giving and its imperfect tense shows that it is ongoing, 'I kept
bestowing', 'I kept lavishing'. *largibar* is a metrically convenient
alternative form of the imperfect (normally *largiebar*).

26 de prono … sinu – this phrase has troubled commentators because of the ambiguity regarding whose the *sinus* in question is. It could be the 'fold' of Propertius's garment, in which he has been carrying his gifts and from which they repeatedly (**saepe**) fall as he bends over Cynthia's bed (the fold is *prono*, 'downward sloping' because of his stance) or the 'lap' of Cynthia, into which Propertius places his gifts, but from which they roll out since Cynthia is lying asleep (now Cynthia's position, lying on her side, explains why her lap is *prono*). Both interpretations have their exponents. The latter, that it is Cynthia's lap, has some attractiveness given that the pentameter usually elaborates the preceding hexameter: just as in 25 the ingratitude is diplomatically transferred from Cynthia to sleep, so here any offence of thanklessness is attributed to the accident of her sleeping position.

27 raro duxti suspiria motu – *duxti* is a shortened form of *duxisti*; the perfect tense contrasts with the preceding imperfects to convey the startling suddenness of this action: 'stirring every now and then, you heaved a sigh'.

28 obstupui – again the perfect tense contrasts with the preceding imperfects in pointed apprehension, 'I was dumbstruck'. **vano credulus auspicio** gives the reason for Propertius's anxiety: he takes the sigh for an omen, though it is an empty one (*vano*).

29–30 – tell us for what Propertius thinks the sigh is an omen. The construction is that of a fear clause, *ne* + subjunctive, '(afraid) that …', and the fearing is implied in Propertius's starting at a suspected omen.

29 ne qua … visa – 'that any visions', the subject of the fear clause.

30 – a second fear clause and an alternative fear (**neve quis** = 'or that anyone'). To translate **invitam … esse suam**, we need to supply a second person pronoun, 'you to be his against your will'.

**A
Level**

31 diversas ... fenestras – it seems now accepted that this means 'parted window shutters' (with *fenestra* able to stand for the opening as well as for what fills it).

31–2 – the epanalepsis of **luna** focuses our attention on the moon that passes by the window. **sedula** personifies the moon as over-zealous – reflecting rather how Propertius perceives it in anticipation of its effects on Cynthia (and in contrast to Propertius's care in not waking her). **moraturis luminibus** is a further personification: the light of the moon is seen to want to linger at the sight of Cynthia. The pentameter (32) furthermore acts out its meaning: just as the light of the moon would linger, so this verse halts the progress to the effects of the moonlight.

33 patefecit – finally the verb of which *luna* is the subject: 'opened'. Now we can understand Propertius's calling her *sedula* (32), 'over-zealous': she wakes up Cynthia, whom *he* has taken so much care not to wake. **compositos** carries meanings of 'closed', 'sealed' and 'settled at rest', which are all appropriate here. **compositos ... ocellos** is elegantly split to the ends of the verse, suggesting the penetration of the moon's rays in their opening.

34 sic ait – this is an abrupt transition to the last portion of the poem, where Cynthia herself speaks. The change to first person for her, from the third person in the beginning of the poem, and then the second person address by Propertius as he presents the gifts, completes the progress from the idealized and mythical to the more immediate and real mistress – but only after a shift to the third person here (*ait*) just before she begins to speak. With **in molli fixa toro cubitum** Cynthia rises to rest on her elbow when she speaks: 'she fixed her elbow on the soft couch' (*cubitum* is accusative of respect, she is *fixa*, 'fixed to the spot as to her elbow').

35–6 – commentators disagree on what *iniuria* (35) refers to. According to one interpretation, Cynthia supposes that Propertius has been rejected by some other woman he has been courting, and so *iniuria* would be used by her sarcastically as 'scorn', 'rejection': 'has a rejection finally, bringing you back to our bed, expelled you from the locked door of another (woman)?' Alternatively, it can be taken in the sense of 'offence' going with *nostro lecto*, 'offence to our bed' (i.e. a metaphor for 'another woman' who is an insult to their love): 'has an offence to our bed finally, bringing you back, expelled you from the locked doors of another (woman)?' The ambiguity and shift between metaphorical and literal in these verses may intentionally echo similar shifts in the beginning of the poem.

37 namque ubi – 'for where (else)' shows that Cynthia cannot think of any other reason than an affair for Propertius's absence from **longa meae ... tempora noctis,** literally 'long hours of my night'. *meae noctis* indicates 'of a night that was my due', 'of a night that you should have spent with me'. **consumpsti** is a syncopated form of the perfect indicative *consumpsisti*, 'you have spent'.

38 languidus – 'limp', here has explicitly sexual associations, and this verbal echo (like many others) recalls the beginning of the poem, opening up the possibilities for alternative meanings there. **exactis sideribus,** 'when the stars have set' (*exactis* = literally 'driven out'), i.e. the whole night is gone, emphasizes how late Propertius has dallied with another (in Cynthia's view).

39 o utinam . . . perducas – Cynthia's wish (or a curse) for Propertius, hence the subjunctive *perducas*, 'may you pass'.

41–2 modo ... / rursus – these indicate alternating times for her activities, 'now (I did this), and then again (something else)'.

41 purpureo . . . stamine – literally 'by purple thread', i.e. by spinning, or weaving with, purple thread. A picture of a very faithful Cynthia: spinning and weaving were the cardinal virtues of a proper Roman *matrona*, a married lady. Furthermore, one cannot fail to think of

A Level

Penelope, the archetypal faithful wife who kept her suitors waiting with the trick of undoing at night the shroud she was weaving during the day. This allusion then personifies sleep and casts him as Cynthia's suitor.

42 Orpheae carmine ... lyrae – *carmine* is ablative of means modifying *fallebam*, 'cheated with a song'. *Orpheae lyrae* is genitive, but most naturally rendered with *carmine* as 'with a song on an Orphean lyre'. Calling her lyre 'Orphean' is not merely an ornamental touch, but carries a pointed meaning. Orpheus was himself an archetypal mourner for a love lost: his bride, Eurydice, died on their wedding day, and Orpheus's attempt to bring her back from the underworld failed through his own mistake. For the rest of his life he rejected women, but his musical performances enchanted all around him. Finally Thracian Bacchants, although initially attracted to him and his music, tore Orpheus to pieces because he rejected them.

44 – gives us the content of Cynthia's complaints (hence the indirect statement with accusative *longas moras*, though the infinitive *esse* is suppressed). **externo ... in amore**, literally, 'in foreign, strange love', 'in love of another': *externus* refers to something alien to what belongs to one, such as one's family. The 'love of another' would therefore refer to affairs Cynthia assumes Propertius has with others. An alternative interpretation would be that Cynthia acknowledges that *theirs* is an extra-marital affair, and *externo in amore* would mean 'in unmarried love', taking the specific meaning of *externus* as outside of one's family. Either way, Cynthia is complaining about the long delays (*longas moras*) common in such an unsettled love affair as theirs.

45 – the expression of this verse is very compressed, and while arriving at a satisfying translation may not be overcomplicated, it opens up different avenues for interpretation. **dum** = 'until'. **me ... lapsam**, 'me, having fallen', 'me, having slipped', refers to Cynthia, the object of **sopor**'s action of **impulit. iucundis . . . alis** could be an ablative of means describing the action of *impulit*, 'pushed with pleasant wings', or ablative of description qualifying *sopor*, 'sleep with pleasant wings'. The verse could then be rendered either as 'until I slipped and sleep pushed me over with his pleasant wings' or 'until I slipped and sleep of pleasant wings pushed me over'.

46 cura – commentators disagree as to the interpretation of this word. It can mean 'cure' or 'treatment', with *lacrimis meis* taken as its indirect object, 'cure for my tears'. Alternatively, *cura* can refer to 'care', 'cause for anxiety', in which case *lacrimis meis* would be 'for my tears', i.e. 'care for me as I was crying'. Taking *cura* as 'cure', *illa* would refer to the preceding line and sleep overtaking Cythia, i.e. curing, or releasing her from her worries. Following the interpretation that *cura* = 'care', 'cause for anxiety', however, *illa* presents further ambiguities: it could refer back to *moras*, the delays in love that Cynthia complains about in 44, or simply to the previous line and her chagrin at not having been able to resist Sleep, her suitor.

**A
Level**

2.14

Propertius has spent the night with his mistress: this poem is his jubilant outpouring at his success in love. The girl is nowhere named in this poem, however, and we are left wondering whether it is Cynthia or someone else.

The poem begins with four mythological *exempla* of rejoicing after a long wait, which are contrasted with Propertius's even greater joy (1–10). Next, he takes a look at his previous dejection as he builds up to the revelation of the key to success in love: indifference (13–20). Propertius then presents his success as equal to a military triumph, culminating with a mock dedication of thanks addressed to Venus (21–8). The tone changes at the end of the poem, however. In the final pair of couplets (29–32), the poet addresses his mistress and shows himself to be at her mercy: the continuation of the happiness depends on her.

1 Dardanio . . . triumpho – 'triump over the Dardanians' (literally, 'Dardanian triumph'); Dardanus was the ancestor of the Trojan royal house, and his name is used metonymically for the Trojans as a whole. **Atrida** (nominative singular), 'son of Atreus', is Agamemnon, who led the Greek army to victory against the Trojans in the Trojan War, which lasted ten years. Alternatively, it can mean his brother Menelaus, for the sake of whose wife, Helen, the war was fought.

2 magnae Laomedontis opes – Troy was proverbially wealthy, hence *magnae opes*, 'great wealth'. Laomedon was the king of Troy under whose auspices the city walls were built.

3 errore exacto – 'when his wanderings were over'. **Ulixes** is a Latin name for Odysseus, one of the heroes of the Trojan War and the eponymous hero of Homer's *Odyssey*, the story of his journey home to Ithaca. It took him ten years to reach home after the war because he was buffeted at sea by angry gods.

A Level

4 carae . . . Dulichiae – Odysseus longed to be home, hence *carae*, 'dear'. *Dulichia* is a poetic alternative for Ithaca, Odysseus's home island.

5 nec sic Electra . . . cum – we may supply an expression for rejoicing on the model of the previous two couplets, e.g. 'not so happy was Electra, when . . .'. Electra was the daughter of Agamemnon and sister of Orestes. Upon his return from Troy, Agamemnon was murdered by his wife Klytaimnestra. Orestes had been sent away before this and he was away for twenty years. The final *a* in *Electra* is here long, as in Greek.

6 cuius falsa . . . ossa – 'whose (i.e. Orestes') pretended bones': *ossa* refers to the bones gathered from the funeral pyre to the urn. They are *falsa*, 'pretended', 'supposed', because Orestes, returning in disguise, brought an urn that allegedly contained his ashes and reported his own death. Electra was deceived by this and mourned him like a dutiful sister, but eventually rejoiced when she recognized him and was let in on the secret. Propertius's poem follows Sophocles's version of the events in his *Electra* (1119–231).

7 nec sic . . . Minois . . . vidit – as with Electra, we may supply an expression of happiness: 'not with so great happiness did Ariadne see. . .' (literally 'not so did Minois see'). **Minois**, 'daughter of Minos', refers to Ariadne, who helped Theseus kill the Minotaur and find his way out of the labyrinth with the help of thread to retrace his steps.

8 Daedalium . . . iter – 'Daedalian path' is the labyrinth, built by Daedalus; it can be expanded to 'his way through the labyrinth of Daedalus'. **lino . . . duce** is an ablative absolute, 'with linen thread as guide'.

9 – brings us out of the similes and gives us the point being illustrated, but the grammar does not parallel that of the *exempla* neatly. The lack of parallelism may reflect the lover's elation. **quanta ego . . . collegi**

A
Level

gaudia, 'as great joys as I recalled', loosely correlates with the expressions of rejoicing in the mythological *exempla*.

10 immortalis ero . . . talis erit – the internal rhyme and play on forms of *esse* gives the verse punchy conclusiveness. **altera**, viz. *nox*, 'another night'.

13 – the subject in this verse (and of *quaerit*) is 'she', the mistress. **nec iam** = 'no longer'. **fastus** is a poetic plural, modified by *iniquos*, 'unfair scorn', the direct object of *opponere*. In English, however, it is better to make 'me' (in Latin, the indirect object **mihi**) the direct object: 'to oppose me with unfair scorn'.

14 mihi ploranti – 'at my crying'. **lenta** here = 'unmoved', 'indifferent'.

11 demissis . . . cervicibus – poetic plural, where the literal 'necks' are better rendered with 'with bowed head'. **ibam**, literally 'I used to go', is more naturally translated with **supplex** as 'I used to be a suppliant'.

12 sicco vilior . . . lacu – *lacus* is any hollow to contain water or wine, such as a vat, basin, cistern, lake or pond: 'worth less than a dry vat (or cistern)' seems a good expression to exemplify uselessness.

16 condicio – 'terms'. **cineri nunc medicina datur**, a hyperbolic expression for a solution found too late: *cinis*, 'ashes', stands metonymically for a dead man that has been rendered to ashes on a funeral pyre, and so 'medicine is now administered to man already dead and buried'.

17 caecis . . . nobis – dative of reference, but most naturally translated as 'the path shone before my feet in my blindness'. The contrast of blindness and the shining of the path in **caecis lucebat semita nobis** makes the irony of the situation more pointed.

18 insano nemo in amore – the word order elegantly reflects the message: the mad love physically embraces the lover on the page as it cloaks his eyes in life.

A
Level

20 sic – 'by doing so'. **veniet**, 'will come', can also mean 'will comply', whether it is about her coming to the lover, or admitting him to her house. **si qua**, literally 'if any', here 'whosoever'.

21 pulsabant alii – the poet speaks of his rivals for the attentions of his girl as locked-out lovers; with *pulsabant*, we are to supply a door: 'others were beating at the door'. **dominamque vocabant** shows the rivals in *servitium amoris*: 'they were calling her mistress'.

22 mecum habuit positum lenta puella caput – the meaning of *lenta* is playfully ambiguous: it can mean, as at 14, 'unmoved', 'indifferent' (i.e. to the rivals banging at the door), but at the same time there is an idea of relaxation in bed clinging to her lover. She has her head (*caput*) literally 'placed with me' (*mecum ... positum*), but to give more meaningful sense, we can render it with 'the indifferent girl rested her head on my chest' or 'the girl clung to me with her head on my chest'.

23 haec mihi potior victoria – supply *est*: 'this victory is greater for me'. **devictis . . . Parthis** is ablative of comparison after *potior*, literally 'than conquered Parthians', but to keep the English more natural, perhaps better 'than the conquest of Parthians'. The Parthians were a warlike people with whom the Romans had fought and who had humiliated the Roman army on two occasions in the first century BC. Under Augustus, however, they were finally brought into line and this was celebrated with images of conquest on coins from the period. A victory over them would therefore be a great and desirable feat indeed, so we are to understand that Propertius's private love conquest has heroic proportions for him.

24 – **haec** refers back to *victoria* in the previous line, and although it is the subject, the verb **erunt** has been attracted to the number of the earlier predicates (*spolia . . . reges*); it can still be translated as singular, however. **spolia . . . reges . . . currus** are all elements in a triumphal procession: the spoils of war displayed in it, the conquered kings paraded before the victorious general, and the triumphal chariot of the general himself. This is the poet's celebration of triumph: 'this (victory) for me will be my spoils, captive kings, my triumphal chariot'. The anaphora of *haec* gives the tricolon forceful rhythm, and further emphasizes the value to Propertius of the victory (*haec victoria*) from the previous verse.

25 – the poet turns to address Venus, calling her by her epithet Cytherea from the island where she was born, Cythera. **magna ... dona** are the accusative plural object, while **tua columna** is a local ablative, 'on your column'. The practice of dedicating votive offerings to express thanks to a god for a favour was common, but here it also continues the theme of the triumph and subverts it: a triumph would culminate in dedicating the spoils to Capitoline Jupiter – and such a triumph was the pinnacle of a Roman aristocrat's career ambitions – but the poet makes his offering to Venus.

26 taleque ... carmen erit – a dedicatory inscription might accompany the offering, and Propertius's is a poem: 'and such a poem will be (inscribed)'.

27–8 has pono ante tuas tibi, diva, ... aedes / exuvias – *has* modifies *exuvias* in the next line, and *tuas* modifies *aedes*, governed by *ante*: 'I place these spoils before your temple for you, goddess'.

28 tota nocte – as at 1.1.7, the ablative of 'time within which' is used for duration, 'for the whole night'. **receptus amans** describes *Propertius* in the previous line, 'received as a lover'.

29–32 – these last two couplets seem to present a very contrasting tone to the jubilation of the poem thus far – to the point that some prefer to see it as a separate poem: there is hesitation and doubt about the future happiness of the poet. Such pessimism, however, is not

**A
Level**

uncharacteristic of Propertius, nor has the poem thus far been entirely void of hints of uncertainty about how long his happiness is to last.

29 – here Propertius turns to address his girlfriend: **mea lux**, literally 'my light', is a term of endearment such as 'my dear'. There is some uncertainty about the manuscript transmission of **ad te**, and emendations have been suggested. However, the meaning is clear enough: 'it depends on you'.

29–30 veniatne ad litora navis / servata, an mediis sidat onusta vadis – this double indirect questions gives us what it is that depends on Propertius's mistress. The metaphor of the ship of love has precedents in Greek poetry and here Propertius applies it to himself: 'whether my ship comes safely to shore, or sinks, freighted, in the middle of the shallows'.

31 aliqua . . . culpa – 'by some fault', though there is some ambiguity as to whose this *culpa* is, Propertius's or his mistress's, and this may be intentional. **nobis**, following **mutabere** (alternative future form, 'you will be changed'), is here naturally rendered as 'towards me'.

32 – the word order neatly illustrates the situation described: the lover will lie dead in the middle of the scene, **vestibulum . . . ante tuum**, 'before your entrance'. The subjunctive **iaceam** is either potential or conditional, 'I should lie', or a prayer, wish or curse, 'may I lie'. The latter could be an assertion of his fidelity and an invitation for his girlfriend to lock him out to die at her doorstep if he proves otherwise – or a threat to place all blame, should he die from heartbreak, upon his mistress.

A Level

Tibullus

1.1

Tibullus's opening poem leads us into a reverie of idyllic country life on his ancestral farm. He contrasts it with the life of a soldier, not only full of hardships of military campaigns, but also, it is implied, motivated by greed. The contrast is, therefore, not only aesthetic in its elegiac rejection of warfare, but also moral, and fits in with the pacifist mood shared with his contemporaries. The first half of the poem (1–40) shares motifs of idealized country life with Horace *Epodes* 2 (though not its tone or irony) and Virgil's *Georgics* and *Eclogues*. For Tibullus, however, the country ideal remains a dream (as indicated by the subjunctive and future verbs), and we learn that he has been or is a soldier. With an address to his patron Messalla (53), with whom we see him campaigning in 1.3, the life of a soldier receives a more positive treatment – only to be dismissed, however, for that of the lover.

In the second half of the poem (45–74), love is introduced into Tibullus's country ideal, but unlike in Propertius 1.1, it is not given the same prominence. The life of the lover, too, is contrasted positively with that of the soldier – Tibullus uses the theme of *militia amoris*, as well – and his wishes focus on life and death with his mistress, Delia. The two halves of the poem are bridged by a passage linking the themes of modest country life to that of love with the mistress (41–4). A concluding section (75–8) ties together the different threads of love, country living and rejection of the life of a soldier into a unified statement of philosophy.

1–6 – these verses form a priamel, a conventional device where the speaker lists common or expected objects of desire (here, wealth and the military lifestyle that leads to it) only to dismiss them in favour of his preference, which is mentioned last: Tibullus's ideal of meagre but relaxed existence in the country.

1 divitias – emphatically placed, and as in Propertius 1.1, the first word of the first poem in the collection has a programmatic significance. Rather than wealth itself, however, it is the *rejection* of wealth and the moral objection to the concomitant greed that form a pervading theme in Tibullus's collection. Money (or gold) and land, which Tibullus immediately brings up in the poem, are traditional measures of wealth. **fulvo . . . auro** is either instrumental ablative with **congerat** or ablative of material with **divitias**; *congerat* is subjunctive with a meaning combining ideas of wish and command: 'let someone else heap up wealth in yellow gold for himself'.

2 culti iugera magna soli – 'great acres of tilled land'. *iugerum* is a Roman measure of land; the English 'acre' conveys the idea (even though it is larger). *culti* indicates that the land is valuable since it can produce crops.

3 labor – 'toil', is commonly used for the hardships of military service, such as fighting, marching, digging trenches, etc. The juxtaposition of the adjectives **adsiduus vicino** underscores the constant presence of danger and exertion in the soldier's life.

4 cui – refers back to the 'someone else' in 1, and it is dative of disadvantage, but most naturally rendered in English as possessive 'whose dreams' (*somnos*). **Martia ... classica pulsa**, literally 'the having-been-struck Martial trumpets', can be rendered into more natural English as 'the blast of the military trumpets'. *classicum* was a military trumpet used by a commander to give signals in battle. *pello*, normally 'strike' with musical (string or percussion) instruments, can also indicate the producing of the sound, hence 'call' or 'blast'.

AS

5 me – contrasts with 'someone else' (*alius*, 1). In **mea paupertas . . . traducat**, 'may my poverty transfer', Tibullus wishes for himself a very different life from that of a soldier, although *traducat*, as a military term for transferring troops, continues the military metaphor. *paupertas* is more accurately 'humble means' than outright poverty, as is also clear from the rest of Tibullus's description of his ideal.

7–8 ipse . . . / rusticus – the words are emphatically placed and highlight Tibullus's personally taking care of the farm. It would be unusual for someone of his standing to undertake the tasks of farming himself (compare Horace's use of a farm manager in his *Epistles*). Given that *rusticus* usually carries a disparaging tone, these words underscore the ideal of simplicity. In the context of the wholesome country idyll, *rusticus* gains a positive sense of moral uprightness in contrast to the seedy city.

7 maturo tempore – here 'in due season'.

8 facili . . . manu – *facili* means 'expert', 'practised': 'with practised hand'. **poma** are here 'fruit-trees'.

9 nec Spes destituat – 'and may Hope not desert me'. Hope is personified as a goddess, and her association with the farmer is traditional. *destituat* may continue the military metaphor: the farmer, like the soldier, has key allies.

10 pleno pinguia musta lacu – 'rich new wine in brimming vat'.

11 nam veneror – 'for I pray': the present indicative verb amidst all the subjunctives and future indicatives emphasizes Tibullus's adherence to traditional worship. *nam* points to the connection between his piety and good harvest.

11–12 seu stipes habet . . . / seu . . . florida serta lapis – 'wherever a tree-stump . . . or a stone has garlands of flowers'. These are the places where Tibullus performs his rustic worship: the tree-stump and stone are likely boundary markers and so may refer to the Roman god of boundaries, Terminus.

13 quodcumque . . . pomum – *pomum* is here 'fruit': 'whatever fruit'. **annus** is here 'season'.

14 libatum . . . ponitur – *libatum* refers to the *pomum* in the previous line, 'is placed as an offering'. **agricolam . . . deum**, 'the farmer god', is a vague expression and may be purposely so. If Tibullus has a specific god in mind, it may be Silvanus, who, elsewhere in poetry, is shown receiving first fruits (e.g. Horace *Epist.* 2.17–22), or possibly Vertumnus. Offering the first fruits to the gods was a common and traditional practice, and the farmers' piety in doing so a standard feature of the praise of the countryside in rhetorical exercises.

15–16 Ceres – an old Italian goddess of corn, identified with Demeter. **rure** is here in the sense of 'farm', 'estate'. **corona / spicea**, 'a crown of wheaten spikes', is a gifts of thanks for the harvest.

17–18 ruber custos . . . / . . . Priapus – Priapus was a fertility god with a large phallus, whose red-painted statues served as scarecrows. The sequence of the complex sentence (**ponatur . . . / terreat ut**, where *ut* should be taken before *terreat*, the subjunctive of the purpose clause) can be rendered into natural English as 'Priapus would be set up as a red sentry . . . to scare. . .'. **terreat . . . saeva** are mock heroic. *terreat* perhaps recalls the horrors faced by the soldier in 3, drawing a humorous contrast between them and the 'horrors' of the countryside – especially when we reach the final word of the line, *aves*: Priapus scares mere birds.

19 felicis quondam, nunc pauperis agri – *felicis* is here 'prosperous': 'of a once prosperous, now poor farm'. Tibullus does not tell us the reason for the decline of his ancestral farm, but indicates this fact with its current smaller size (22) and its greater prosperity in his forefathers' time (41-2).

20 custodes . . . Lares – the Lares were the guardians of the whole estate, and here probably the *Lares compitales* are meant, the protectors of crossroads and so the surrounding fields. **fertis** is here used in the sense of 'accept an offering', and with **munera vestra**, 'receive your gifts'.

21-2 – the reference is to the annual ritual purification of the land and its produce by a sacrifice, called *lustrum*. In **vitula . . . lustrabat caesa**, the imperfect verb has the sense of habitual action in the past, 'a sacrifice of a young heifer used to purify'.

22 agna exigui est hostia parva soli – a lamb was a poor man's offering, and so reflects the impoverished state of Tibullus's farm: 'a lamb is the little victim for my meagre land'.

22-3 agna . . . / agna – anaphora is typical of bucolic and elegiac poetry – and so suits the countryside setting – and may also imitate here the language of prayers.

24 clamet: 'io messes et bona vina date' – *clamet* is likely a jussive subjunctive, 'let the country folk shout'. *io* is a ritual exclamation, best kept as it is when translating the direct speech, and *bona* can be taken with both *messes* and *vina*, although it agrees grammatically with the latter only: 'io, give good crops and wine'.

25 iam modo, iam possim – *modo* used in a wish (with subjunctive) means 'if only', and the emotional repetition of *iam* make this an emphatic wish, 'now, if only now I might'.

26 deditus – a military metaphor of being delivered up, surrendered (*dedo*): 'not be delivered up (*deditus esse*) to the long

AS

road'. The 'long road' (*longae* . . . *viae*) represents one of the hardships facing soldiers, and this is our first indication that Tibullus is or has been one.

27–8 – the *locus amoenus* (a 'pleasant place') of a shade under a tree by a river is a commonplace of literature, and a prominent feature of bucolic poetry (e.g. Virgil *Ecl.* 7.10–13), well suited for characterizing Tibullus's country ideal.

27 Canis aestivos ortus – 'the summer rising of the Dog-star'. *Canis* is the Dog-star (Sirius), which rose shortly after the summer solstice and is commonly used in poetry as a metonym for the intense heat of the height of summer.

29 nec . . . pudeat tenuisse bidentem – rendered into more natural English by exchanging a personal construction for the impersonal *pudeat*: 'I would not be ashamed to hold a mattock'. *pudeat*, literally 'it would cause shame', like *pigeat*, 'it would irk' (31), indicate that these tasks could be seen as being below a 'civilized' man of Tibullus's standing (and continue the theme of overcoming the aversion to humble tasks of farming begun with *rusticus* in 8). *tenuisse* (and *increpuisse* in the following line) is a perfect infinitive where we might expect a present. The perfect infinitive is metrically convenient, but it may here also recall the early Latin use of the perfect infinitive after verbs of wishing or prohibiting; simply metrical considerations are unlikely to dictate choice here and a suggestion of the ideal of good old times may be present.

30 stimulo . . . increpuisse – usually *increpare* refers to verbal correction, so its use here with *stimulo* suggests both verbal and physical urging of the sluggish oxen: 'to reprimand' or 'to rebuke with the goad'.

31–2 – more natural English is achieved by replacing the impersonal *pigeat* with a first-person construction: 'I would not be displeased (*non . . . pigeat*) to carry home (*referre domum*) in my lap (*sinu*) a lamb or the young of a goat (*agnamve . . . fetumve capellae*) left behind (*desertum*) by a forgetful mother (*oblita matre*)'. The repeated *a* sound in these verses may suggest bleating. We may compare with this Virgil *Ecl.* 1.13–15, where there is another abandoned kid.

35–6 hic ego . . . / . . . soleo – the logic of *hic* is to give the reason why the thieves and wolves should look elsewhere (i.e. *de magno . . . grege* in the previous line): 'for here it is my habit/custom to'. **quot annis** = 'each year'.

36 placidam . . . Palem – Pales was an old Roman goddess who protected flocks and shepherds. She was offered only non-blood libations, and milk was one of the earliest rustic offerings, a detail suggesting the traditional piety of the scene.

37 adsitis, divi – 'come, gods'. It was traditional in prayers to ask for the presence and participation of the gods. The archaic form *divi* adds to the solemnity of the prayer.

37–8 neu vos e paupere mensa / dona nec e puris spernite fictilibus – 'do not scorn (*neu vos . . . spernite*) gifts (*dona*) from either a poor table (*e paupere mensa*) or from clean earthenware vessels (*nec e puris . . . fictilibus*)'. *mensa* here is a sacrificial table. *puris*, in addition to the requisite ritual cleanliness, carries the morally positive suggestion of 'unadorned', 'simple'. Earthenware vessels likewise point to the morally upright simplicity of the country dweller, as they are inexpensive.

39–40 fictilia . . . / pocula – here *fictilia* is an adjective modifying *pocula*, 'earthen cups'. **antiquus primum sibi fecit agrestis** ('the ancient rustic was the first to make for himself') provides us with the other symbol of morality for Romans in addition to the countryside: ancient times. Tibullus's defence of earthenware here draws on these ideas. In **de facili composuitque luto**, -*que* should be taken first, and *facili* here means 'easy to handle', 'malleable': 'and formed (them, i.e. the earthen cups) from malleable clay'.

41–2 patrum . . . / . . . antiquo . . . avo – while *patrum* in the plural refers to 'ancestors' in general, the singular *avo* could refer to Tibullus 'grandfather' in particular, though some commentators prefer to take it as parallel to *patrum* and as 'ancient forefather'. **condita messis** = 'stored up harvest'.

44 solito – 'customary', 'familiar' (as opposed to the constant change experienced by a soldier) describes **toro**, 'on a familiar bed'. **membra levare**, literally, 'to lighten (my) limbs', but more naturally in English 'to rest my limbs', again draws a contrast with the soldier, who would be carrying a heavy pack on marches.

45 quam iuvat cubantem – begins an exclamation on the joys of the country ideal of Tibullus: 'how pleasant it is for the one who is lying in bed'.

46 dominam – the first mention of Tibullus's mistress and the first indication of love in the poem. *domina* also suggests the theme of *servitium amoris*. **tenero . . . sinu**, 'in a tender embrace', contrasts with *immites* in the previous line, as well as with the toughness of the soldier. **continuisse** = 'to hold tight'.

47 cum fuderit Auster – 'whenever the South wind pours'. The South wind is traditionally associated with rain and storms. He is described additionally as **hibernus**, 'wintry', to magnify the harshness of the weather.

48 securum – 'carefree', is still accusative following *iuvat* in 45 and describes the person for whom it is pleasant **somnos . . . sequi**, 'to pursue dreams', 'go on sleeping carefree'.

49 hoc mihi contingat – the subjunctive expresses a wish, and with dative the verb means 'befall one', 'be one's lot': 'may this be my lot'.

A S

sit dives, likewise a subjunctive expressing a wish, begins a contrast with the different lot of the soldier, 'may he be rich'. **iure** = 'by right', 'rightly'.

49-50 furorem / qui maris et tristes ferre potest pluvias – the relative pronoun *qui* should be taken before *furorem* in translating the clause: 'who can bear (*qui ... ferre potest*) the frenzy of the sea (*furorem ... maris*) and the gloomy rain (*et tristes ... pluvias*). The dangers of seafaring are a traditional *topos,* and connected to gaining wealth: the implied greed of such pursuits gives seafaring negative moral connotations.

51-2 – quantum takes the partitive genitive (*auri* and *smaragdi*; the *-que* in *potiusque* is best taken with *smaragdi*); a natural translation is achieved with 'o, may all the gold and emeralds in the world perish (*o quantum est auri pereat ... -que smaragdi*) rather than (*potius ... / quam*) any girl (*ulla puella*) cry (*fleat*) on account of my travels (*ob nostras ... vias*)'. **vias** here refers to the soldier's campaigns on which riches might be gained. The double consonant at the start of **smaragdi** does not cause the preceding syllable to be scanned as long.

53 Messalla – Tibullus addresses his friend and patron, who is from a distinguished Roman family, *gens Valeria,* and himself distinguished in several military victories. With reference to Messalla, the theme of warfare is treated in a positive light in terms of the glory it can confer: **te bellare decet,** 'waging war becomes you'. **terra ... marique,** 'by land and sea', is a traditional military phrase emphasizing the extent of his service and glory.

54 – a purpose clause showing the reason for Messalla's waging war: to bring glory to himself and his family. **domus** is here his 'town-house', and it was customary to hang spoils of war in the *vestibulum* in recognition of the victorious general's achievement: 'so that your town-house may sport enemy spoils'.

55–6 – Tibullus draws a contrast between Messalla, the active, glorious soldier, and himself, the inactive lover (*te*, 53 and *me*, 55) and the doors associated with each: Messalla's door decorated with spoils (54), and that of the elegiac mistress decorated with the shut-out Tibullus (56). **duras ianitor ante fores** picks up the *topos* of the locked-out lover: *ianitor*, 'door-keeper', makes the poet-lover the slave of his girlfriend, and the epithet *duras* is here applied to the doors instead of the harsh mistress: they are physically hard, but also suggest their owner's hard-heartedness.

57 Delia – as Tibullus turns to address his mistress, we finally learn her name.

57–8 tecum / dum modo sim, quaeso segnis inersque vocer – *dum modo* begins a proviso clause, 'provided I am with you'. *quaeso … vocer*, literally, 'I ask to be called' (*vocer* is present passive subjunctive in an indirect command, in prose constructed with *ut* + subjunctive), may be rendered with 'please all call me'. *segnis* and *iners* are military words of disapproval, 'cowardly and unwarlike'.

60 deficiente manu – an ablative of means, literally, 'with a failing hand', but more naturally in English 'in my failing arms'.

63–4 non tua sunt duro praecordia ferro / vincta, nec in tenero stat tibi corde silex – 'your breast is not bound in hard iron, nor is there flint in your tender heart'. *praecordia* are literally the muscles before the heart (*prae corde*), but often, as here, used for 'heart', 'breast' as the seat of emotions. There is a play here with *praecordia* and *corde* as well as the idea of the doors locking the lover out before which Tibullus is bound (55–6). Iron and flint are traditional images for a lack of feeling (compare e.g. Cic. *Tusc.* 3.6.12, Ovid *Met.* 9.614, *Am.* 2.5.11).

65–6 – 'from that funeral (*illo … de funere*) no young man (*non iuvenis … quisquam*), no maiden (*non virgo*) will be able (*poterit*) to

return home (*referre domum*) with dry eyes (*lumina . . . sicca*)'. *lumina
. . . sicca* is the object of *referre*, literally, 'to bring back dry eyes'. Young
men and girls as mourners increases the pathos of this funeral, but
they are also the appropriate audience and appreciators of the elegiac
poet and *praeceptor amoris*.

67–8 manes – were the deified spirits of the dead. Untying and tearing
or cutting hair and tearing one's cheeks were traditional gestures of
lament, but Tibullus does not want Delia to spoil her beauty in this
way for his sake.

69 iungamus amores – with the jussive subjunctive *iungamus*,
Tibullus turns to exhort love for his mistress and himself while they
are young, 'let us join in love'.

70–2 – give the reason why they should indulge in love now: soon
enough old age and death come to make love inappropriate or
impossible (compare e.g. Cat. 5). **iam** here is 'soon'.

70 tenebris – can modify either **veniet**, 'will come in darkness', or
adoperta, 'covered with shadows', or it may be taken to apply to both.
Mors, 'Death', is personified in a striking image: nighttime is the
traditional time for love, during which the lover (or the mistress)
might come in the darkness to his beloved, but here an end to it is
imagined with Death taking over this role.

71 subrepet iners aetas – 'idle old age will creep up': just as Death will
come by stealth, so does old age – and hence there is a suggestion of
urgency to enjoy the present.

72 cano ... capite – 'when one's hair is white', a common
circumlocution for old age. Here the idea of what is becoming (as
earlier with the soldier, 53) is picked up and applied to love: in old age,
sweet-talking (*dicere blanditias*) is inappropriate.

AS

73 nunc levis est tractanda Venus – *levis* is 'light' both in the sense of 'carefree' and 'fickle', 'changeable', and also a term designating the lighter genre of love elegy (as opposed to weighty epic). *tracto*, a military term for conducting warfare, suggests the theme of *militia amoris*, though the verb can also be used for 'handling' a subject as a writer: 'now light Venus is our duty/subject' (literally, 'now light Venus is to be conducted/handled'). **frangere postes**, 'to break the doorposts', is an occupation of a locked-out lover.

74 inseruisse – 'to insert' or 'introduce' into the usual interactions of the lovers, that is, 'to start'. Brawls, like besieging the door of one's mistress, are typical actions of the lovers in elegy.

75–8 these concluding verses sum up the themes of the poem (love, warfare, the ideal of modest countrylife) and return to the initial image of the riches in ring-composition.

75 hic ego dux milesque bonus – makes the theme of *militia amoris* explicit: it is in the fields of love (*hic*), not of war, that Tibullus excels.

75–7 vos, signa tubaeque / ite procul, cupidis vulnera ferte viris, / ferte et opes – *signa tubaeque*, 'the standards and trumpets', stand metonymically for warfare. They are given different commands in the field of love: 'deal wounds (*vulnera ferte*) to greedy men (*cupidis ... viris*), and bring them riches, too (*ferte et opes*)'. These orders continue the theme of greedy acquisition of wealth through warfare (where *viri* can be footsoldiers): Tibullus wishes to be far away from it all and in the fields of love instead. In the latter, however, *viri* may also carry the sense of 'husbands'. Tibullus wishes them to be far away, too, so as not to stand in his way in his affair with his mistress. There is thus a double pun, as not only *vir* but also *cupidus* can have two meanings: greedy for wealth as well as sex.

77 ego composito securus acervo – *composito . . . acervo* explain how Tibullus is to be *securus*, 'I, at peace, with my heap (of corn) stored away'.

78 dites despiciam despiciamque famem – the chiastic ordering of line elegantly sums up Tibullus's position of superiority (*despiciam*, 'may I look down on') in his ideal of modest means between riches and famine.

1.3

This poem stems from a particular occasion: Tibullus's falling ill while accompanying Messalla on official business (some commentators date this to shortly after the battle of Actium in 31 BC). His unhappy circumstances spark a meditation on love and death, the evils of the war-torn present and the happiness of the Golden Age. The poem's progression reflects the wandering thoughts of a sick man, as it moves from reality to dream, present to past and future, skilfully creating a sense of the feverish visions with elegant transitions between each.

The poem opens with an address to Messalla, sailing off on campaign while Tibullus is left behind (1–8). Thoughts of having no one there to mourn him should he die lead him to reminiscences of Delia at their parting and an appeal for help to Isis, whom Delia worships (9–34). A contrast with his preferred traditional Roman gods leads him to look back longingly on the blissful Golden Age (35–48), which he sets against the Iron Age under Jupiter that now seems to bring on his death (49–56). Thoughts of dying provoke a contemplation of a happy afterlife in Elysium for faithful lovers (57–66) and punishments in Tartarus for his rivals (67–82). The poem concludes with a vision of Delia spinning late into the night at the moment of Tibullus's joyous homecoming to her (83–94).

1–2 – the beginning of the poem adapts the genre of *propemptikon*, a send-off poem wishing the traveller a safe journey, but Tibullus then quickly transitions to a meditation on his unfortunate situation. Elements of the *propemptikon* pervade the poem, however, although they are focused not on the traveller but on the poet himself (e.g. signs for a safe voyage, evils of sailing, homecoming).

1 ibitis – 'you will go', is plural, since besides Messalla in this line, it is addressed to his *cohors* in the next (*ipse cohorsque*).

A
Level

2 o utinam – expresses a wish (made emphatic by *o*), though the verb is supressed, 'o, if only you yourself and your company may remember me'. **cohors** (i.e. *cohors praetoria*) refers to Messalla's retinue on his tour of duty, of which Tibullus, too, has been a part.

3 me ... aegrum – here we learn why Tibullus is left behind: he has fallen ill. **Phaeacia** is the place where Odysseus is shipwrecked on his journey home in Homer's *Odyssey*, and the island was later identified with Corcyra (modern Corfu). Tibullus's choice of the Homeric name suggests a comparison with Odysseus.

4 abstineas ... Mors modo – the verb is a jussive subjunctive addressed to the personified *Mors*, 'Death'. In **avidas ... manus**, the proverbial greed of Death is transferred to her hands.

5–8 – in a Roman funeral, when the pyre had burnt out, the bones were gathered by the chief mourners and sprinkled with wine and milk. They were then mixed with perfumes and spices and placed in an urn in a sepulchre.

5 non hic mihi mater – *mihi* is a possessive dative, 'here I do not have a mother'.

6 quae legat – *legat* is subjunctive in a relative purpose clause, 'to gather'. **in maestos ... sinus** may be either 'in mourning bosom' or 'in the folds of a funerary dress'. The enclosing word order of **in maestos ossa perusta sinus** neatly illustrates the enclosing of the bones in the *sinus*.

7 non soror – to be constructed like *mater* in 5, with *hic mihi* understood, '(here I have) no sister'. **quae dedat** is another relative purpose clause, 'to give', or given the context, perhaps better 'to mix'; *fleat* in the following line is likewise a subjunctive in the relative purpose clause, 'to weep'. **Assyrios ... odores**, 'Assyrian perfumes': perfumes imported from Syria were particularly prized, with 'Assyrian' generally used for 'Syrian' in poetry.

A Level

9 Delia non usquam – like the mother and sister, Delia is absent in this foreign place: 'no Delia anywhere at all'. The thought of her prompts a change to looking back at the moment of departure from Rome: in translating **quae me cum mitteret urbe**, it is best to start with *cum* and change the relative pronoun *quae* into a personal one, 'when she was letting me go from the city'.

10 ante – adverbial: 'beforehand', 'first' (i.e. before letting Tibullus go).

11 illa sacras pueri sortes ter sustulit – 'she thrice drew the sacred lots of the boy'. Divination by lot was a common way of seeking advice on a given course of action, such as setting on a journey. *sortes* were tablets inscribed with an ambiguous message, shuffled in a container and usually drawn by a boy (but here Delia does it herself), and then interpreted by a *sortilegus*, a professional fortune-teller. Delia draws the lots three times (*ter*), because three is a sacred and lucky number. **illi** (dative singular) refers back to Delia, 'to her'.

12 rettulit e trinis . . . puer – 'from each of the three (*e trinis*) the boy reported'.

13 cuncta dabant reditus – *cuncta* refers to the consultation of the gods, lots and omens and *dare* is here used in the sense of 'foretell': 'they all promised a return'. (Maltby's text has a misprint, *dabunt* for *dabant*.)

13–14 tamen est deterrita nusquam / quin fleret . . . respiceretque – 'yet she was not at all kept from crying and regarding with anxiety'. **nostras . . . vias** refer (as at 1.1.26) to the marches of the soldier.

15 cum iam mandata dedissem – *mandata* are the final instructions given right as one leaves, i.e. Tibullus is on the point of leaving, 'when I had already given my parting instructions'.

16 quaerebam . . . usque – the imperfect tense of *quaerebam*, 'I kept seeking', and the adverbial use of *usque* in the sense of 'always',

'constantly' emphasize Tibullus's ongoing attempts to stay. In **tardas**
. . . moras, *tardas* has an active meaning of 'delaying', 'slowing': Tibullus
seeks 'hindrances to delay me'.

17-18 aut ego sum causatus aves aut omina dira / Saturnive sacram
me tenuisse diem – the two instances of *aut* should be taken with
aves and *omina*: 'I pleaded as an excuse that either birds or evil omens
(*aut . . . aves aut omina dira*) or the sacred day of Saturn were holding
me back'. The *aves* are birds of omen consulted upon embarking on a
journey and taken here to give unfavourable signs. *Saturni diem*, 'the
day of Saturn', is a reference to Saturday, the Jewish Sabbath, which
some Romans following the custom of Jews may have regarded as
unpropitious for greater undertakings. Alternatively, it may be an
astrological reference, as Saturn was considered a baleful planet, and
days under his influence unlucky.

19-20 – stumbling at the treshold at the start of a journey was
considered a particularly bad omen. **mihi** is to be taken with **dixi**, 'I
said to myself' or **dedisse**, 'that stumbling (*offensum . . . pedem*,
literally, 'dashed foot') in the gateway (*in porta*) had given me an
unlucky sign (*tristia . . . signa*)'. **tristia** is used of warning signs, hence
the meaning 'unlucky' here.

21-2 – this couplet gives the moral of the story: Amor punishes those
who disobey. **invito . . . Amore** is an ablative absolute with *esse*
suppressed, 'against Amor's will' (literally, 'with Amor being unwilling').
audeat . . . ne quis . . . / aut sciet egressum se 'if anyone should dare
. . . and he will know that he has set out'. *aut* here has a meaning of 'and'
rather than 'or', and emphasizes the result of knowing from his
suffering that he has broken against a god.

23 tua . . . Isis – 'your Isis', the Egyptian fertility goddess introduced to
Rome in the time of Sulla. Despite official resistance to her cult, she
steadily gained popularity and was worshipped particularly by

A
Level

women, especially foreigners and courtesans; hence Tibullus's use of *tua*, and contrast with his preference to worship the traditional Roman Penates and Lares (33–4). **prosunt** is plural because it has as its subject not only Isis in this line but also *aera* (24), *lavari* (25) and *secubuisse* (26), 'what use now to me are your Isis . . ., what use to me that *sistrum* . . ., or what (use) your bathing . . . and sleeping apart . . .'.

24 illa tua totiens aera repulsa manu – *aera* here refers metonymically to the *sistrum*, the 'rattle' usually made of brass used while praying to Isis, 'that *sistrum* so often shaken by your hand': Delia used to pray to Isis on behalf of Tibullus and shake the *sistrum* as a part of the ritual.

25–6 – the worship of Isis included ritual bathing (*lavari*) and sexual abstinence (*secubuisse*), both of which were to be done with ritual purity (*pure*, 'cleanly', *puro . . . toro*, 'in a chaste bed'). The sexual abstinence lasting usually 10 days and nights was particularly bothersome to the lover-poet, hence the rueful **memini**, 'I remember (all too well)'.

27–8 nam posse mederi / picta docet templis multa tabella tuis – Isis was known for her powers of healing, and as such is an appropriate deity for the ill Tibullus to turn to. Those healed by the goddess would hang votive tablets illustrating the cure (*picta . . . tabella*) in her temple as thank-offerings (compare Juvenal 12.27–8). With *posse*, we need to supply *te*: 'for many a painted tablet in your temples proclaims that you can heal'.

29–32 ut . . . / . . . sedeat / . . . debeat – this is somewhere between a purpose and a consecutive clause, common in prayers, 'help me . . . and Delia shall sit . . .'.

29 votivas . . . voces – is a periphrastic expression for *votum*, a promise to a god to do a given thing in return for a favour, which, upon receiving the favour, one would fulfil (*persolvens*): 'fulfilling her vows' (literally, 'fulfilling her votive utterances').

A
Level

30 lino tecta – 'wearing linen', another symbol of purity in the worship of Isis.

31 resoluta comas – *comas* is accusative of respect, literally, 'loosened as to her hair', but in better English 'with her hair unbound'.

32 insignis turba . . . in Pharia – Delia with her unbound hair would stand out (*insignis*, 'notable') among the mass of worshippers of Isis, whose priests had shaven heads – but there likely is also a suggestion of her outstanding beauty. *Pharia*, 'Pharian', is metonymical for 'Egyptian' because of the lighthouse of Pharos at Alexandria.

33 mihi contingat – as at 1.1.49, 'may it be my lot'. **Penates** were Roman gods associated with the home and, like Lares, traditional Italian gods worshipped by a family from generation to generation. There is a contrast between Tibullus's established Roman gods and Delia's foreign goddess. There is also a wish to return home, since Penates and Lares were associated with homecomings.

35 – after the transitional couplet on the inherited gods (33–4), Tibullus moves on to contemplate the happiness of life in the Golden Age under Saturn, another traditional Italian god. According to the myth of the ages, there was no seafaring or need for agriculture in the Golden Age, as earth offered its fruit of its own accord, and men lived in peace. This was succeeded by gradually deteriorating Silver, Bronze and Iron Ages. Often, as here, only two of the ages are mentioned: the ideal of the past Golden Age contrasted with the present time under Jupiter, which was marked by wars and dangerous seafaring caused by greed.

37 pinus – used metonymically for 'pine-wood ship': the first ship, Argo, was made of pine and the symbol for the beginning of the decline from the Golden Age (compare Cat. 64). The idea of the moral superiority of the Golden Age over the present time colours the description throughout. In this verse it is built into **contempserat**, 'had defied', 'had scorned', suggesting the hybristic crossing of the boundaries of one's lot: neither pines nor men belong at sea.

38 effusum . . . sinum – refers to the fold of the sail, 'billowed sail'.

39 vagus – describes *navita* in the next line, as does **repetens compendia**, 'seeking profit', 'bringing back gain', which explains his motive: this, too, carries a negative moral tone.

40 presserat – here, 'had weighed down'. **externa . . . merce**, 'with foreign wares', like *ignotis terris* in the previous line, further emphasizes the unnaturalness and foreignness of this activity.

41–2 – **non** does not negate *validus* but the entire sentiment, 'at that time, no strong bull bent under the yoke', that is, there was no agriculture or subjugation of animals. The last idea is expanded to horses in the next line with **domito . . . ore**, 'in its tamed mouth': without tame horses, there was no long-distance travel either, as such travel as was done had to be done on foot.

43 non domus ulla fores habuit – an innovation on the Golden Age theme: there was no need for doors as there were no thieves – but also importantly for the elegiac lover-poet, he could not be locked out either.

43–4 non fixus in agris / qui regeret certis finibus arva lapis – the antecedent *lapis* should be brought up front in translating, and *est* supplied with *fixus*. The relative clause is one of purpose, and *regere fines* is a legal phrase for marking boundaries: 'no stone was set in the fields to measure off the plough-land with fixed boundaries'.

45 ipsae . . . ultroque – 'of themselves . . . of their own accord', these words convey the idea that in the Golden Age nature provided of its own accord for all the needs of man.

45–6 ultroque ferebant / obvia securis ubera lactis oves – literally, 'and of their own accord (*ultroque*), ewes (*oves*) brought (*ferebant*) udders of milk to meet (*ubera lactis obvia*) carefree people (*securis*), but more natural English can be achieved with something like 'of their own accord, ewes offered their udders full of milk to the carefree people they met with'.

48 duxerat – 'had drawn out', i.e. 'had moulded', 'had forged'. Besides the absence of warfare caused by anger, there was no metalworking, and most notably, no production of weapons in the Golden Age.

49–50 – the anaphora of **nunc** brings us back to Tibullus's day and the Iron Age under Jupiter. We need to supply 'there is' in translating, 'there is slaughter, wounds…'. Although **repente** is an adverb, 'suddenly', **leti mille repente viae** is most naturally translated as 'a thousand roads to sudden death'.

51–2 – Tibullus is afraid that his current sufferings are a result of divine punishment, but maintains that he has not committed perjury. **timidum** can be interpreted as either '(because I am) god-fearing', or concessive, 'although I am afraid', and balances **non me periuria terrent,** 'it is not perjury that causes my fear'.

53 quod si – 'but if'. **fatales** here is 'fated', i.e. the years allotted by fate.

54 fac lapis . . . stet – the omission of *ut* after an imperative of *facio* is common in periphrastic commands, 'set up a stone'.

55–6 – the epitaph, a characteristic motif of elegy, serves as a transition to the contemplation of Elysium.

55 immiti – here in the sense of 'unripe', 'untimely', 'premature', in addition to 'ungentle', 'harsh', 'savage', the meaning it has at 48.

56 terra . . . sequiturque mari – the displaced -*que* coordinates *terra* and *mari*, for the traditional military phrase (see 1.1.53). The epitaph compliments Messalla, the poet's addressee in the beginning of the

A Level

elegy, while at the same time suggesting that the evils of the modern age are the cause of Tibullus's death.

57–8 – the Elysian fields appear in literature as early as Homer's *Odyssey*, but making it a place for lovers with Venus taking over the role of Mercury as the guide of the souls – a special favour to the lover-poet – may be Tibullus's invention. **quod** = 'because'. **facilis** is here = 'susceptible to', 'open to', 'compliant'.

59 choreae – the *e* in the second syllable (usually long) is here scanned as short, *chŏrĕae*.

59–60 – the repetitive sound quality of the lines with *-que vigent . . . -que vagantes / . . .-ce sonant* is attractive and reflects the sense. In **tcnui gutture**, *tenuis*, 'tender', suggesting gracefulness and charm, marks the birds' throats and so their singing as elegiac and Callimachean.

61–2 fert casiam non culta seges . . . / . . . terra benigna – Elysium has much in common with the Golden Age, as here with earth producing fruit without cultivation. *casia* is a tree with an aromatic bark, probably the wild cinnamon. *seges* here is 'land', 'soil', and *benigna* 'rich', 'fruitful', 'fertile'.

63–4 – in Elysium, the blessed continue to pursue their occupations in life, so here the lovers engage in neverending amatory play. **series** = 'row' (or 'line', 'rank', looking forward to the military metaphor in the following line). **ludit**, 'plays', frequently indicates amatory play, lovemaking and also the writing of poetry (compare Cat. 50.2), or any combination of them. The military phrase **proelia miscet** brings us to the sphere of *militia amoris*, the only kind of warfare in Elysium.

65 illic est cuicumque . . . amanti – 'here is to whomsoever . . . when he was a lover', i.e. who were lovers at the moment of their death. **rapax** points to the proverbial greed of Death (like *avidas*, 4).

A Level

66 insigni . . . coma – 'in his distinguished hair', that is, the lover's hair is distinguished by the myrtle, sacred to Venus.

67 at scelerata . . . sedes – to contrast with Elysium of the faithful lovers, Tibullus paints a picture of the abode of the wicked in Tartarus as a destination for his rival.

69 Tisiphoneque – Tisiphone was one of the Furies, spirits of vengeance tormenting the wicked. In **impexa feros pro crinibus angues,** *feros . . . angues* is accusative of respect with *impexa*, literally, 'uncombed as to the savage snakes in lieu of hair', or in more natural English, 'unkempt with savage snakes for hair'.

69–72 – the sibilance and *x* in *impexa* suggest the hissing of the snakes of Tisiphone and Cerberus.

71–2 Cerberus – was the monstrous guard hound of Hades, usually represented with three heads, and, as here, with snakes bristling on his head and neck (as well as sometimes on his tail). **serpentum . . . ore / stridet,** i.e. Cerberus has the serpents in his mane hiss at the wicked. *ore* is a poetic singular for the plural of the snakes' mouths.

73–80 – the list of the wicked punished in Tartarus is a common literary theme, and Tibullus singles out four famous examples.

73–4 – Ixion, the king of the Lapiths, tried to rape Juno and was punished by being bound to an ever-revolving wheel. The participial phrase in **Iunonem temptare Ixionis ausi / . . . noxia membra** is easiest rendered with a relative clause, 'the guilty limbs of Ixion who dared to make an attempt on Juno'; *temptare* carries its erotic connotations here.

75–6 – Tityos attempted to rape Leto and as punishment he was stretched out and had vultures feed on his liver. He was a Giant, and hence was spread **novem per iugera terrae**, 'over nine acres of land'. **viscere**, 'with his entrails', stands poetically for 'liver', a suitable target as it was thought to be the seat of the passions.

77–8 – Tantalus divulged the gods' secrets, killed his son Pelops and served his flesh to the gods, but it may be that a crime against love is intended here. According to one story, he raped Jupiter's cup-bearer Ganymede; this would form a neat parallel to the other assailants of Jupiter's favourites, as well as a suitably learned allusion for the elegiac poet. Tantalus was also variously punished, but Tibullus focuses on his standing in a pool of water which recedes each time he tries to quench his thirst. **circum** is used adverbially, 'around him (are pools of water)'. **acrem**, describing **sitim**, can be both 'severe', 'fierce' and 'eager', and so personifies the thirst. The repetition of **iam iam** emphasizes the immediacy of being on the point of drinking, further underscored by the future participle **poturi**.

79–80 – The daughters of Danaus, except for Hypermestra, violated love (hence **Veneris quod numina laesit**) by murdering their husbands on their wedding night. They were punished by having to carry water in leaking vessels into a leaking container, an endless task. **quod** = because. **cava** is here 'perforated', 'full of holes'. **Letheas**, 'of Lethe', the River of Forgetfulness, was one of the rivers of the underworld.

81 illic sit quicumque – Tibullus wishes his rivals to end up in this part of the underworld. **violavit** has the sense of 'profaned', 'desecrated', as love and lovers are sacrosanct (compare with *sanctique pudoris* in 83). **amores** may refer to 'love' or 'beloved' – the latter would refer specifically to Delia.

82 lentas ... militias – Tibullus suspects that his present delay on military service is the result of a curse by a rival. *lentas* is here 'slow', 'long-lasting'.

A Level

83 – the thought of the rival leads Tibullus to address Delia with an appeal for how he would like her to be. **casta**, as often in elegy, is here 'faithful' (compare Prop. 1.1.5 and see note).

83–92 – the domestic scene is reminiscent of Terence *Heautontimoroumenos* 275–307, where a lover learns of the quiet way his faithful mistress has spent her life in his absence. Spinning at home is the task of a chaste Roman matron *par excellence*, and there may be a suggestion of casting Delia as a Penelope to Tibullus's Odysseus stranded in Phaeacia (3). Cynthia represents herself in a similar way in Prop. 1.3.41–6.

84 adsideat . . . sedula . . . anus – the old woman as a companion and adviser of the mistress is traditional, though she does not always guard her mistress's virtue (*sanctique pudoris / . . . custos*, 83–4).

85 fabellas referat – storytelling was a part of such occasions; *referat* is subjunctive as this is all part of Tibullus's wish, 'she would tell'. The work could go on late at night, hence **positaque lucerna**, 'when the lamp had been lit'.

86 – the wool was held on a distaff (*colus*), and the thread (*stamen*) drawn off (*deduco*) from it to a spindle, 'she would draw down long threads from a laden distaff'.

87 circa – adverbial, 'around her'. *pensum* is a portion of wool weighed out for each spinner; that they are 'heavy' (**gravibus**) indicates the tedium of the task and Delia's steadfastness. **adfixa** here is 'intent on', and **puella** is collective singular for the plural of Delia's maids: 'around her, the maids intent on their heavy allotments of wool'.

88 fessa remittat – these go with *puella* in the previous line, 'tired, would slacken', 'would relax'.

89 tunc veniam subito – Tibullus's sudden homecoming brought out in rapid dactyls contrasts with the slow spondaic pace of the scene of spinning. It was customary to have one's arrival announced ahead of time, but Tibullus returns unannounced (**nec quisquam nuntiet ante**), either to test Delia and find out how she spends her time in his absence, or outright trusting that she has been faithful and has nothing to hide (compare how Lucretia, spinning late into the night, wins the 'contest' of the virtue of a Roman *matrona* when her husband drops in unannounced in Livy 1.57).

90 videar caelo missus – these words suggest a supernatural epiphany, and *caelo missus* is a proverbial phrase for something unexpected, usually positive.

91 qualis eris – in addition to showing her haste to meet Tibullus, Delia's casual appearance shows that she has been faithful as she has not dressed up for another lover.

93–4 hunc illum . . . / Luciferum – 'this day (*hunc . . . Luciferum*), the one I have been describing (*illum*)', where the more remote *illum* suggests this day is yet to come. *Lucifer*, the Morning-star i.e. Venus, can be used in the sense of 'day', as the star that marks the start of the day: its name means 'Light-bringer'. **Aurora** is the goddess of Dawn, and her Homeric epithet 'rosy-fingered' may have suggested the colour of her horses here, **roseis. candida** (describing Aurora), besides the colour, connotes brightness, beauty and good fortune, as can **nitentem**. The poem ends with a note of light and optimism in contrast to its beginning with darkness and desperation (*Mors . . . nigra . . . / . . . atra*, 4–5).

A Level

Ovid *Amores*

1.1

In this programmatic poem, Ovid announces his subject matter and genre through a clever variation on *recusatio*, a formulaic refusal to write grand epic. The model derives from Callimachus *Aitia* 1.1, where he declines to write about kings because Apollo commands him to keep his Muse slender (adapted in Virgil *Ecl.* 6, Prop. 3.3, Horace *Odes* 4.15; see introduction). In Ovid's case, however, the god commanding the poet is Cupid, who steals a foot of Ovid's verse (see note on 3–4 below) and the *topos* is treated with humour and full awareness of his literary predecessors: Ovid expects his reader to be *doctus*, 'learned', and recognize the many allusions to the literary tradition in which he places himself. The poem also prefigures his attitude to love that pervades the collection: rather than a passionate and earnest lover, he is playful and witty, often making fun of himself as the lover (sometimes he even makes fun of the conventions of the genre in a cold and calculating way, e.g. 2.8, 19). In fact, here he has no beloved – he is poet first, lover second. We should keep in mind that the *recusatio* need not be taken seriously – and Ovid's humorous treatment of it certainly does not suggest that we should.

The poem opens with Ovid telling us that he has prepared to write epic but through Cupid's intervention, ended up writing elegy (1–4). He then complains to Cupid about the boy-god's presumption in transgressing into Apollo's realm, and gives several *exempla* about gods taking over each other's prerogatives to argue for the absurdity of such an enterprise (5–20). Cupid responds by shooting an arrow of love at Ovid, which makes the poet a lover (21–4), and Ovid has no choice but to acquiesce and bid farewell to epic (25–30).

1 arma . . . bella – the opening recalls Virgil *Aeneid* 1.1 *arma virumque cano* and the epic's second proem in book 7 (esp. *dicam horrida bella*, 7.41), suggesting heroic war as Ovid's subject as well. **gravi numero**, 'weighty rhythm', designates the form of epic, often signalled by words such as *gravis*.

2 materia conveniente modis – this refers to the idea that different metres are appropriate for different subjects. *modis* is here 'metre'.

3–4 par erat inferior versus – in hexameter used for epic, the second, 'lower' (*inferior*) verse is of equal length to the first, but in elegy, although the first verse is a hexameter, the second is a pentameter, one foot shorter (see note on metre in the introduction). Hence the fact that Cupid is said **unum surripuisse pedem**, 'to have snatched one foot', forces Ovid to write elegiac couplets.

5 iuris – partitive genitive with *hoc*, 'this right'.

6 Pieridum vates – *Pierides* were the Muses, goddesses inspiring poetry. This name for them derives from Pieria on the northern slope of Mount Olympus, the place of their birth (Hesiod *Theogony* 53). Alternatively, it is the patronymic of 'the daughters of Pieros', a Macedonian king; they were identified with the Muses. *vates* is a dignified term for a 'poet', originally meaning 'prophet'. It was adopted by the Augustan poets to indicate the solemnity of their calling, and is especially appropriate for epic poets.

7–12 – in these verses Ovid presents an argument against Cupid's usurping Apollo's prerogatives in terms of imagining paradoxical reversals of gods' roles.

7 quid si praeripiat – 'what (would happen) if . . . would snatch away'. *praeripiat* is subjunctive in the protasis of a remote conditional (the apodosis is understood from *quid*, as expanded above). Minerva is the goddess of crafts and wisdom, as well as a warrior goddess often represented in armour (identified with the Greek Athena).

8 ventilet . . . faces – torches are symbols of love and so appropriate to Venus (see Prop. 1.3.10 and note), but wholly incongruous with the virginal Minerva.

9–10 Cererem . . . / . . . pharetratae virginis – Ceres, the mother-goddess of agriculture and open fields is contrasted with another virgin goddess, Diana, of the mountain glades and hunting, indicated through her attribute of the quiver (*pharetra*). **lege,** 'under the rule', like *iuris* in 5, indicates the power or jurisdiction of a given deity.

11 crinibus insignem . . . Phoebum – Phoebus is an epithet of Apollo, notable for his long, uncut hair, a sign of his eternal youth. *crinibus* is an ablative of respect with *insignem*. **cuspide** is a metonym for spear.

11–12 – since Apollo is not entirely unwarlike (although Mars is proverbially unmusical), the contrast here is more between the attributes of the two gods: the spear and the lyre stand for war and peace. There is also wordplay: **movente lyram** recalls the expression *arma movere*, 'wage war'. Instead of a sharp spear, we might expect the god of poetry to have *acutam vocem*, 'a clear voice', playing with the two meanings of *acutus*. **Aoniam,** 'Aonian', modifying *lyram*, refers to the region in Boeotia where the home of the Muses, Mount Helicon, was located.

15 an, quod ubique, tuum est? – this elliptical expression can be expanded out to *an id, quod ubique est, tuum est?*, 'or is everything everywhere yours?' (literally, 'or is that which is everywhere, yours?'). **Heliconia tempe** = 'Heliconian valley'. *tempe* is a Greek neuter plural; originally, Tempe was the name of a valley near Olympus, but later came to be used as a generic term for any valley. Helicon is the haunt of the Muses.

AS

16 vix . . . iam – 'hardly any longer'. **Phoebo** is a dative of reference with **tuta**, and **sua** refers back to him, 'his (own) lyre is assured to Phoebus'.

18 attenuat nervos . . . meos – *nervos*, literally 'sinews', but often, as here, 'vigour', 'power'. It indicates the forcefulness of Ovid's literary work and his ability as a poet – he was attempting epic. *attenuat*, 'weakened', 'lessened', 'made slight' acknowledges the weakness of the pentameter comparative to the hexameter (**proximus ille** = 'that next one', i.e. verse, understood from *versu* in 17; the *inferior versus* in 3), but also suggests the Callimachean ideal of *tenuitas*, slenderness.

19-20 – Ovid complains that he has no appropriate subject matter (**materia**) for writing elegy since he is not in love: he has no beloved boy or girl (**aut puer aut . . . puella**). Poets such as Catullus, Horace and Tibullus had composed poems for beloved boys in addition to their mistresses. **numeris levioribus**, 'for lighter rhythms', refers to elegy (in contrast to the weighty epic) and echoes the opening couplet. *levis*, like *tenuis*, forms part of the technical vocabulary referring to the kind of poetry that conforms to the Callimachean ideal. **longas . . . comas** is accusative of respect with **compta** (modifying *puella*), literally, 'combed as to her long hair', but better 'with long combed hair' – she is sophisticated (on hairdressing, see *Am.* 2.8.1 and note).

21 questus eram – the pluperfect emphasizes the conclusion of his speech. **phraretra . . . soluta** is an ablative absolute, where *solvo* is used in the sense of 'undo', 'open': 'having opened his quiver'. **cum protinus** brings home the ability of the divinity to accomplish his purpose quickly and easily: the inverse *cum* construction (we might expect 'when I had complained, he. . .) contributes to the effect.

22 in exitium . . . facta meum – this construction, *in* + accusative, expresses purpose, 'made for my ruin'. **spicula** is metonymical for 'arrows'.

AS

23 fortiter – with reference to drawing the bow, the adverb indicates physical strength.

24 quod … canas … opus – *quod* is a relative pronoun referring to *opus*; placing the relative clause before its antecedent emphasizes the delayed *opus* and suggests the tension as Cupid draws the bow. *canas* is subjunctive in a relative purpose clause, 'for you to sing'. **vates** mockingly recalls the poet's own designation of himself (6).

25 me miserum – the accusative of exclamation marks the moment Ovid is transformed into a love poet. The phrase is common in Roman comedy for young men blocked from their objects of love and much used by Ovid and, to a lesser extent, Propertius. The words may also recall Prop. 1.1.1.

26 uror – Cupid's arrow instantly brings on the metaphor of fire for love common in elegy. **in vacuo pectore** wittily conveys the paradox that Ovid is consumed by love even though he does not have a beloved yet (19–20) – a striking contrast to the earlier elegists.

27 sex … numeris, in quinque – *sex* and *quinque* both modify *numeris*, and the postponed *in* governs it, 'in six feet … in five (feet)'. **surgat** and **residat** are both jussive subjunctives, 'let rise … let fall', and reflect the idea of rise and fall in the elegiac couplet, with its first verse, the epic and so more 'manly' hexameter, rising and the weaker and decidedly elegiac pentameter falling (compare 17–18).

28 – the poet bids farewell to epic in a way that recalls the opening of the poem in neat ring-composition: with *ferrea … bella* compare *violentaque bella* in line 1, and *modis* occurs in the same place both here and in 2.

29 litorea flaventia tempora myrto – the chiastic word-order plays out the meaning: the the blond temples are bound by myrtle from the seashore on the page, as well. The entire hexameter is made of five words, considered particularly elegant and so makes the address to the Muse particularly dignified.

29–30 – at the close of his programmatic poem, Ovid turns to address his Muse (**Musa**, vocative singular), now to be marked with emblems of love elegy: myrtle is sacred to Venus and the elegiac couplet is made of eleven feet (six of the hexameter and five of the pentameter). **cingere** is a passive imperative used reflexively with an accusative of respect, **tempora**, 'wreathe your temples' (literally 'bind yourself as to your temples'). **emodulanda** is an Ovidian coinage, combining the idea of measuring off with melodiousness.

AS

2.5

By *Am.* 1.3, the poet-lover has acquired a beloved, and the poems begin to explore their relationship. The second book of the collection delves into some more serious trouble in paradise that the life with a mistress entails – though in a typically Ovidian manner, this, too, is treated humorously. Making fun of himself, or more precisely, of his poetic *persona*, Ovid plays with the incongruities in the position of the traditional elegiac lover. He exploits not only a frequent elegiac setting for flirtation, the dinner party, but also his own poetry: this elegy contains many echoes of the advice he gives his mistress to use against her husband at a dinner party in *Am.* 1.4, but now she uses it against her lover.

The sequence of the poem is as follows: I wish to die because you have been unfaithful (1–4); I wish my case against you were not as good (5–12); but with my own eyes I saw you with another man at a dinner party when you thought I was asleep (13–28); I shout out against her, claiming what is mine (29–32); her reaction and blush are described in similes – she is more beautiful than ever (33–44); I want to attack her but her beauty defends her, and I ask for kisses instead (45–50); she kisses me all too well – I am pained as she must have been taught by another (51–62)!

1 tanti – genitive of value, 'worth so much', leading to the result clause in the following line (*ut. . .*).

3 te peccasse – Ovid addresses his mistress (unnamed in the poem, but presumably Corinna), who has wronged him. *peccasse* is the contracted perfect active infinitive, and the verb, as often in elegy, has the meaning of 'to be unfaithful'.

4 in mihi perpetuum . . . malum – the construction is accusative of purpose with *in*, and *mihi* is dative of disadvantage (naturally translated as possessive): 'for my never-ending torment'.

5 deceptae . . . tabellae – wax tablets to convey the lovers' messages are a recurrent feature of elegy. *deceptae* has posed problems for interpreters, but likely means here 'disguised', 'camouflaged'.

6 munera – gifts were customary in courtship (compare Prop. 1.3.24–6). **crimen habent** is legal terminology, 'give grounds for accusation', and begins the extended legal imagery.

7–8 arguerem – continues the legal imagery, here in the sense of 'I would plead my case', as do **vincere**, 'win one's suit', and **causa**, 'case'; the poet-lover wishes his allegations were unfounded.

9–10 felix, qui . . ./ cui . . . – 'happy he, who . . . (and) to whom . . .', the formula common in solemn contexts is humorous here. **quod amat** i.e. his mistress; Ovid often uses the neuter for the object of affection. **non feci** is a legal phrase, 'not guilty'.

11–12 – the poet thinks the man who insists on proving his mistress's infidelity to be too unfeeling. **ferreus**, literally, 'made of iron', indicates his lack of feeling, and **suo favet ille dolori** that he is too absorbed in his own indignation. **cui** is a dative of agent with the passive verb. In addition to being awarded to victorious generals and athletes, palms could be awarded for forensic victories; that his **palma** is **cruenta** shows that the victory is achieved at an unnecessarily high price to the loser. **victa . . . rea** continues the legal imagery (*rea* = 'female defendant').

13 – Ovid finally gets to the matter at hand, his mistress's infidelity at a dinner party, which he has witnessed himself. Many details from here onwards recall his advice to his mistress in *Am.* 1.4, starting with the unmixed wine intended to lull him into a drunken stupor to keep him in the dark.

14 sobrius apposito . . . mero – the ablative absolute may have a concessive sense here, 'sober, although the unmixed wine was set beside me'.

AS

15-20 – the poet's mistress has agreed on methods of secret communication with the other man: twitching eyebrows conveying messages (**supercilio . . . vibrante**), significant nods (**nutibus**), eyes sending messages (**non oculi tacuere tui**), writing on the table with wine (**conscriptaque vino / mensa**; Maltby's text has a misprint, *conscriptaeque*) and finger language (**in digitis littera**). These are typical of love poetry, and again recall *Am.* 1.4.

18 nec . . . littera nulla – the double negative produces a strong positive in litotes, 'and many a letter'.

19-20 – The poet recognizes their coded language: **sermonem . . . quod non videatur agentem**, 'conversation dealing with what it did not appear to (deal with)'. **verbaque pro . . . iussa valere**, 'and words made to stand for'. **notis** is 'code' and **certis** 'fixed', 'pre-arranged' here.

21 frequens . . . conviva – collective singular, 'guests in great numbers'.

22 compositi – i.e. by wine: 'lulled to sleep by wine', 'drowsy with wine'.

24 illa – neuter accusative plural referring back to *oscula* in the previous line (*lingua* is feminine ablative singular); the parentheses explain why they are *inproba*: they are no innocent pecks, but kisses with tongue. **mihi . . . liquet**, 'it is clear to me that'; *liquet* is a legal term referring to a verdict that is unambiguous, continuing the legal language begun at 6.

25-8 – the multiple similes elaborate the lover-poet's disapproval, and the mythological *exempla* in 27-8 illustrate the generic examples of 25-6 effectively: Diana is both Apollo's sister and a virgin huntress, whereas the adulterous affair of Venus and Mars is a famous scandal – and like the poet-lover, Venus's husband Vulcan witnesses the pair.

25 germana – a more elevated word for 'sister', it also emphasizes the blood-relation and so the point.

26 mollis – a term appropriate to unwarlike elegy, but also 'compliant', 'yielding' of an elegiac mistress. It furthermore contrasts with Diana's rigorous lifestyle of hunting and chastity.

29 – the sudden direct speech effectively conveys the outburst of the lover-poet and the drama is enhanced by the historic present **exclamo. defers** is a somewhat technical term in legal contexts, where it is often used in the sense of 'bestow', 'award', 'confer' benefits.

30 iniciam . . . manus – continues the legal imagery: the phrase echoes the formula of the plaintiff in *manus iniectio*, an archaic legal enactment associated with the process by which a man might reclaim his rightful property from another. **mea iura** likely refers to kisses (rather than his mistress), the property he sees as rightfully his, 'I shall lay my sovereign hands on what is rightfully mine'. The juxtaposition of the solemn, archaic legal process with kisses results in his humorously poking fun at himself.

31 – the antimetabole of the pronouns emphasizes the exclusivity the poet-lover expects of the relationship. **haec** refers back to *gaudia*.

32 in . . . venit – continues the legal language: as a technical term, *venire* + *in* = 'become legally entitled to' (usually of inherited property). **bona** is commonly used in the sense of 'property'.

33 haec ego – the verb of speaking is, as often, omitted, 'I said these things'. The shift from the second to third person for the mistress with **illi** (until 56) distances her to a more mythical existence of enchanting beauty, elaborated in the slew of similes describing her blush.

34 conscia . . . ora – continues the legal theme, 'guilty face'. **pudor** here is her blush of shame. This is an elegant 'golden line' (adjective A, adjective B, verb, noun A, noun B). The assonance of *pu* may suggest the poet-lover's hesitation at the change of heart when he sees his mistress's beauty.

AS

35-40 – the description of the blush recalls Virgil *Aen.* 12.64-9 on Lavinia's blush, which also includes similes with tinted ivory and roses mixed with lilies. The Ovidian simile of a bride blushing at the sight of her bridegroom (36) may echo Lavinia herself, who blushes before his fiancé Turnus. The details of the simile of tinting ivory also recall Homer's *Iliad* 4.141-5, where such a simile illustrates the blood running from Menelaus's wound and likewise has a Maeonian woman performing the tinting.

35-7 quale – adverbial in both 35 and 37, and to be supplied with the similes of the girl seen by her bridegroom, the Moon and the ivory.

35 Tithoni coniuge – ablative of personal agent without *a*; the wife of Tithonus is the goddess Dawn.

38 cantatis ... equis – refers to a lunar eclipse caused by the incantations of witches (see Prop. 1.1.19-24), during which the Moon would redden. She was traditionally depicted with a chariot and horses, and it is these that are now affected by the incantation.

39-40 quod ... / ... ebur – *quod* is a relative pronoun referring to *ebur*, postponed to the end of the couplet (we should take it as *aut (quale fulget) Assyrium ebur, quod...*). **Maeonis ... femina**, 'Maeonian woman'; Maeonia was a part of Lydia, and may stand metonymically for it. *Assyrium* is another example of geographical inexactitude common in the Latin poets, and like at Tib. 1.3.7, may be more indicative of the route whereby the ivory arrived at Rome, most likely from India (like the ivory in the Virgilian simile in *Aen.* 12.64-9).

41 his ... aut alicui ... horum – the prosaic pedantry of 'her blush was very like these, or one of them' deliberately undermines the loftiness of the accumulated similes: an example of the irony on the poet's part.

42 casu – 'by chance' and so here possibly just 'as it happened', or more emphatically 'intentionally', i.e. she does not contrive to look attractive, either by feigning a blush, which could itself be attractive (see *Am.* 1.8.35–6), or by use of make-up.

45–6 – the parenthetical **et erant culti** (here 'elegantly coiffed') is a humorously unexpected turn after *sicut erant*, which usually refers to careless appearance. It continues the poet-lover's admiration of his mistress's beauty amidst his anger, even as he is about to attack her. **fuit . . . impetus** goes with both **ire** (here 'attack') and **laniare**, 'I had an impulse to tear . . . and attack. . .'. Tearing the mistress's hair and cheeks is a recurrent element of the elegiac love-affairs.

47–8 fortes cecidere lacerti – *cecidere* is third person plural perfect indicative active; *fortes* is ironic, given the traditional qualities of the *mollis* elegiac lover. **defensa armis . . . suis** evokes the legal imagery (*defendere*, 9) as well as the *topos* of *militia amoris*.

49 saevus . . . supplex – the stark contrast effectively conveys his dramatic transformation, underscored by the alliteration of *s*. **ultroque** here, in addition to 'of my own accord', has the connotation of 'in contrast (to my previous state)'.

50 oscula ne . . . deteriora – the request, enjambed for the surprise effect, is doubly humorous: after *supplex*, we might except the lover-poet to beg for forgiveness, not kisses. Moreover, he wants them to be no worse than those she has given to his rival.

51 ex animo – 'from the bottom of her heart'.

51–2 qualia possent / excutere irato tela trisulca Iovi – the hyperbole of the simile strengthens *optima*. *tela trisulca* refers to Jupiter's traditionally three-pronged thunderbolt, often hurled as a sign of his anger.

53 – the lover-poet's bliss is short-lived, however, as jealous thoughts trouble him. **ne** begins a fear clause after **torqueor**, 'I am in torment, (fearing that) the other man . . .'.

54 ex hac . . . nota – 'of this quality'; *nota* is used metaphorically from wine-bottling, where it referred to the label that indicated the type, age and quality of the wine stamped on the cask, but then came to be used for a 'mark of quality' more generally.

55–62 – the poet's apprehensions in his role of *praeceptor amoris* provide a twist ending: she has learnt more from someone else!

55 quam docui multo meliora – *quam* follows the comparative *meliora*, 'much better than (those which) I taught'.

56 quiddam . . . novi – *quiddam* takes the partitive genitive, 'something new'. **addidicisse**, 'to have learnt in addition (to what I had taught)' – to his dismay, the pupil has surpassed the master.

57–8 – paradoxically, the ever-so-enjoyable kisses are an evil to the jealous poet-lover. The interlocking word-order (*recepta* to be understood with *tota labellis / lingua tua est nostris*, and *labellis, tota lingua* and *est* with *nostra recepta tuis*) and the antimetabole of 58 reinforce the description of the kisses and their mutual sharing. **placuere** is third person plural perfect indicative active, its subject are the kisses.

59–60 non oscula tantum / iuncta queror – there is innuendo in 'I complain not only that. . .': *non . . . tantum* euphemistically indicates that more is meant than said, and *oscula . . . iuncta* suggests *corpora iungere* (so *oscula* may here be 'lips' rather than 'kisses').

61 – the order in which to take the words is *illa nusquam potuere doceri, nisi in lecto*, 'they could never have been taught, except in bed': the evidence for his worst fears that were conveyed in the innuendo of the preceding couplet.

62 nescioquis – does not need to indicate a man unknown to the lover-poet, but can be used contemptuously of a successful rival. **pretium grande magister habet** continues the theme of *praeceptor amoris*, though now the teacher is someone other than our poet – to his dismay: 'some other teacher has received a substantial price'.

2.7

This poem forms a pair with 2.8. Here, the lover-poet adamantly defends himself before Corinna against charges of sleeping with her maid Cypassis: not only would it be impossible, but also shameful. In 2.8, he addresses Cypassis, who apparently has heard what he has said to Corinna in 2.7. But now that the mistress is not present we find out that the charges were true after all. He flatters the maid and contrary to what he has said to his mistress, shows enthusiasm for their affair. The poems are an exercise in rhetoric demonstrating Ovid's ability to argue both sides of a case. Using the second elegy to show the first in a different light is an example of Ovidian originality, and together they demonstrate amply the hardened, even callous, yet frivolous attitude to love he demonstrates in the collection.

An indignant exclamation on the mistress's charges begins the poem (1–2) and leads to a defence by reference to past accusations that are shown as absurd and so impossible (3–10). The poet-lover then makes use of proverbial ideas in his defence: he wishes for guilt as the guilty bear punishment with equanimity and warns Corinna of the ineffectuality of too much castigation (11–16). Only after this does he address the new accusation of sleeping with Cypassis, which he defends against on account of its absurdity (17–26). The poem concludes with his oath of innocence (27–8).

1 ergo – begins the poem *in medias res*, plunging us in the middle of the row without introduction. **sufficiam reus in nova crimina** introduces the legal flavour of the poet-lover's defence: 'am I to stand trial as a defendant for new crimes' (literally, 'am I to provide sufficient material as a defendant for new accusations').

2 ut vincam – is concessive, 'although I win', and is used in a legal sense (to win one's case), as is **dimicuisse**, 'to have contended'. The form in *-cuisse* is an alternative common in poetry for the regular first conjugation perfect ending (*-avisse*).

3 respexi summa theatri – 'I have looked back at the high (seats) of the theatre': under Augustus, men and women had segregated seating at the theatre, with women relegated to the seats high up at the back of the theatre. Ovid elsewhere teaches that the theatre is a good place to meet a girlfriend (*Ars* 1.89–100).

4 – unde stands for *qua*: 'you choose from the many the one on whose account you want to be grieved'. The placement of the verbs to frame the line emphasize that Corinna's suffering is her own making.

5 candida 'pretty': an adjective of praise indicating brightness or whiteness, and so, beauty. Ovid elsewhere uses it of Corinna herself.

6 tacitas . . . notas – for lovers' secret signs, see *Am.* 2.5.15–17. The repetition of the participle results in witty wordplay: where Ovid sees no expression (*tacito vultu*), Corinna finds furtive signs (*in vultu tacitas . . . notas*).

7 miseros . . . capillos – these are the lover-poet's own (compare Tib. 1.6.69–72).

8 crimen dissimulare putas – we are to understand *me* with *dissimulare*, 'you think I am hiding a transgression'. *crimen* suits the legal tone of the passage (like *culpo*, though here used for criticizing a person's appearance), but it is also a common elegiac term for infidelity.

9 bonus color est – understand possessive dative *mihi*: Ovid looks too healthy to be in love (the opposite is conveyed in the next line with *seu malus*, with which understand *color*). The idea of pallor as a symptom of love has a long tradition; see Prop. 1.1.22 for another example. **in te**

A
Level

quoque frigidus esse is an indirect statement depending on *dicor* in the next line. *frigidus* is here 'cool', 'sexually unresponsive'.

11 atque ... vellem – introduces an emphatic wish resulting from what he has just said, 'and I wish'. **peccati mihi conscius**, 'my own partner in crime' (literally, 'accomplice in crime for myself'); *peccatum* is in elegy often used of infidelity.

12 – 'those who have earned it, suffer their punishment with equanimity'. The *sententia* is intended to prove the poet-lover's innocence by contrast to his remonstrations.

13 insimulas – 'make an allegation'; significantly, it refers more frequently to false accusations than true charges.

15 aspice – introduces a paradigm ('look, how...'): the donkey has been beaten too much for the punishment to have an effect any longer. **miserandae sortis** is genitive of description, 'of pitiable lot'.

17 – more than halfway through the poem, we finally learn what the accusation is this time: that the poet-lover has slept with his mistress's maid. **Cypassis** is a suitable name for an attractive slave-girl, as it transliterates the Greek word *cypassis* for a short tunic that reveals some leg (in contrast to the long dress worn by Roman women).

17–18 Cypassis / obicitur ... contemerasse – the unusual personal passive construction is perhaps intended to convey that Cypassis and the lover-poet are passive victims of Corinna's empty accusations: 'Cypassis is brought as a charge in that she has defiled'. *contemerasse* is a strong word for 'pollute', 'defile'; with the mock-epic *dominae ... torum* it stresses the heinousness of the crime, and so the unlikelihood of its having occurred.

19 di melius – elliptical form of an old prayer-formula (supply *dent*, *faciant* or the like), 'may the gods grant better'. This is the lover-poet's defence from the shamefulness of sleeping with a lowly slave: the gods should grant better than that he would like such a slave as a girlfriend – if he had any wish to be unfaithful to begin with (*si sit peccasse libido*).

20 contemptae sortis – another genitive of description, though *sortis* may here have a slightly different meaning, 'of despised rank'.

20-2 – the phraseological echoes with *sortis* and *verbere* between the descriptions of Cypassis and the donkey (15–16) may suggest that the slave-girl shares the donkey's proverbially lascivious nature.

21 Veneris famulae conubia – *Veneris conubia* stands for 'sexual union' (literally, 'union of Venus'; the phrase comes from Lucretius 3.776) and it takes the genitive for the person with whom it is, 'with a slave-girl'. The legal sense of *conubia* is likely in play, as well: slaves could not contract *conubia* (legal marriage, in contrast to the general *concubitus*, used in *Am.* 2.8.6), underscoring the impossibility of Corinna's accusations. Another way to take the phrase is to understand *Veneris famulae* as going together: *Venus* was used as a term of endearment, 'servile sweetheart', or the phrase could be taken as the paradoxical 'a slave love-goddess', again driving home the preposterousness of Corinna's claims. All these meanings can be simultaneously in play, too.

23 ornandis ... operosa capillis – 'painstaking in arranging your hair'. (Maltby in his text prints *operosa*, but in his commentary has *operata*, an alternative reading.)

24 grata ministra – 'favoured servant'. The elegiac mistress is often conceived as a goddess, and both these words flatteringly support that understanding of Corinna: *ministra* is used of attendants on a deity and *grata* of favour with one.

25 scilicet – makes the rhetorical question sarcastic. The verb (*est*) is omitted in **quae tam tibi fida**, 'who is so faithful to you'. **rogarem** is here, as elsewhere in elegy, used of asking for sexual favours (compare also Cat. 8.13–14).

26 quid, nisi ut – 'why, if not in order that'. **indicio** is a legal term, 'with informing (on me)'. Again, the poet's point is that it would be absurd of him to try to seduce his mistress's favourite maid, for he could count on Cypassis to reject him *and* tell Corinna all.

27 – the poem closes with a lover's vow, which is ironically suspicious: such vows were proverbially worthless. **pueri volatilis**, 'of the winged boy' = Cupid; the meaning 'flighty' for *volatilis* is also implied.

28 – 'that I am a defendant for a crime not committed'. The legal vocabulary links the closing line of the poem to its opening in ring-composition, asserting the close of his case.

2.8

The poet-lover opens with praise of Cypassis to gain her favour, the rhetorical *captatio benevolentiae* (1–4), but swiftly moves on to question her about how Corinna found out about the affair while asserting his own success in covering it up (5–8). A more flattering (and defensive) tone is resumed with recourse to mythological *exempla* to convince Cypassis that he did not mean it when he maintained to Corinna that having an affair with a slave-girl was shameful (9–14). Again, this quickly gives way to blaming Cypassis for giving the game away and his own achievement in hiding it with an oath (15–20). He then asks for Cypassis's favours as a reward for his services, turning to blackmail if she does not agree (21–8).

1 ponendis . . . perfecta capillis – *perfecta* is used in the sense of 'very skilled', 'exquisite in arranging hair'. **in mille modos** because increasingly complicated hairstyles had become fashionable with Roman women.

2 Cypassi – Greek vocative of the Greek name.

3 non rustica – a flattering understatement. Unlike in Tibullus, *rustica* is not a positive term in the urbane poetry of Ovid, where it comes to refer to sexual unsophistication (compare *Am.* 1.8.44, 2.4.13–14): contrary to what he has said to Corinna (2.7.20), Cypassis is no country bumpkin, certainly not when it comes to lovemaking, as the lover-poet well knows (*mihi . . . cognita*). **furto,** literally 'theft', in erotic contexts comes to refer to illicit relationships (see Prop. 4.7.15).

4 apta – the play on different meanings of the word is typical Ovidian wit: Cypassis is suited to Corinna as a hairdresser, but she is better suited to the lover-poet – in bed.

5 inter nos sociati corporis – 'of sexual intercourse between us' (literally, 'of a body associated between us'). **index,** 'informer', like *indicium* in 2.7.26, is a juristic term. The poet-lover turns very factual and official immediately after the flattery of the *captatio benevolentiae*.

6 concubitus . . . tuos – the singular possessive shifts all the blame on Cypassis. **unde** = 'from whom', given that Ovid seems to be trying to identify a person, not other evidence.

7 num tamen erubui? – 'but surely I did not blush?' The poet-lover is drawing a contrast between himself and what he says of Cypassis in 16.

8 furtivae Veneris – *Venus* is here, as often, used metonymically, 'of our stealthy love'.

9–10 – 'what of it that (*quid quod*) I maintained (*ego contendi*) that anyone who (*si quis . . . / illum*) can commit a (sexual) misdemeanour with a slave-girl (*in ancilla . . . delinquere possit*) lacks (*carere*) sanity (*mente . . . bona*)'. *delinquere* has sexual connotations, like *peccare* at 2.7.19, which this picks up; *in* + ablative indicates the sphere where an offence is committed. We may imagine that Cypassis interrupts the poet-lover's positive self-appraisal here, and with this rhetorical question and the *exempla* that follow he attempts to placate her resentment at his argument in 2.7.19–22.

11 Thessalus – 'the Thessalian hero', i.e. Achilles, who loves his captive Briseis in Homer's *Iliad*. **facie . . . arsit** is another instance of the metaphor of fire for love, with the simple ablative for the object of passion, 'burns for the beauty'.

12 serva . . . Phoebas – 'the slave priestess of Phoebus (Apollo)' is Cassandra, a Trojan princess captured by Agamemnon, the 'Mycenaean leader' (**Mycenaeo . . . duci**, dative of agent). Both of the slaves in the *exempla* are high-born captives, which Cypassis likely is not, thereby flatteringly elevating her. At the same time, however, the poet-lover undermines himself: since Cypassis is not such a noble lady, the comparison is somewhat far-fetched. Moreover, Briseis is the

A Level

cause of the quarrel between Achilles and Agamemnon that causes the Greeks much trouble in the *Iliad*, and Agamemnon's wife Klytaimnestra kills him on his return home with Cassandra – the *exempla* are ironic for the poet.

13 Tantalide – 'descendant of Tantalus', i.e. Agamemnon (Tantalus was his great-grandfather); the form is an ablative (of comparison with *maior*), as is **Achille**.

15–16 tamen . . . / . . . te . . . erubuisse – recalls *num tamen erubui* in 7 and so works to fix the blame on Cypassis. The subject of **defixit** is Corinna.

17 si forte refers – 'if perhaps you remember' is a sarcastic reminder of the poet-lover's bravado at 2.7.27–8. **praesentior**, i.e. with regard to his mental abilities: 'more composed'.

18 feci . . . fidem – though uncommon in poetry, the phrase here means 'I induced belief', by swearing by Venus, as we saw him do at 2.7.27–8.

19–20 – that gods do not punish perjured lovers was proverbial, and Venus is often, as here, presented as the forgiving deity (compare *Am.* 1.8.85–6, Hor. *Odes* 2.8.13–14). **animi periuria puri**, 'perjuries of a pure heart', is a delightful oxymoron. They were frequently carried off by winds to signify their worthlessness (e.g. Tib. 1.4.21–2, *Ars* 1.633–4), as here the South winds (**Notos**) are ordered to do. **Carpathium . . . mare**, named for the island of Carpathus, was a notoriously stormy sea between Rhodes and Crete: these perjuries are to be dispelled particularly swiftly.

22 – this line explains what the *pretium . . . dulce* the poet-lover has in mind is. **concubitus . . . tuos**, while echoing 6, is here more positive, 'with you' rather than 'yours', though hardly redeems the accusatory tone of the earlier instance. **fusca**, 'dark', suggests that Cypassis may be

A Level

of African or Asian origin; there was a vogue for such slaves in Rome and they could be expensive (compare Ter. *Eun.* 165–7). The adjective may, however, refer simply to a darker-complexioned white.

23 – the direct address conveys Cypassis's reaction. **quid renuis**, 'why do you refuse': throwing back the head signified emphatic dissent. With **fingis . . . novos . . . timores** the poet-lover accuses Cypassis not of 'imagining' but of 'fabricating' new sources of fear.

24 unum . . . e dominis – the poet-lover speaks as if Corinna and he are masters of the same household and he therefore has rights as owner over Cypassis. **emeruisse**, 'to have gained the favour of', has a double meaning here: generally if it were regarding Corinna, and in a sexual sense regarding the poet (compare 4 and note).

25 index – recalls 5 and marks the return to legal language.

26 veniam – is here more or less synonymous with *esse*, 'I will be the betrayer' (**proditor**). With **culpae . . . ipse meae**, 'of my own guilt myself', the poet-lover finally acknowledges his share in the blame, but at the same time takes his threat to Cypassis to an extreme in a twist ending.

27–8 – the threat to specify the place (**quoque** = 'and in which'), times and manner of the offence recalls forensic language (compare e.g. Cic. *Cluent.* 124), and echoes Tib. 2.6.51–2. The alliteration of the harsh *q* underscores the relentlessness of the blackmailing. **tecum fuerim** is an erotic euphemism (compare *Ars* 3.664). **modis** has a sexual meaning here – in contrast to *modos* in 1 – as 'sexual positions': the ring-composition, too, has a twist in it.

Vocabulary

An asterisk by a word indicates that it is included in OCR's Defined Vocabulary List for AS.

abdo, abdere, abdidi, abditum	hide, conceal
abeo, abire, abivi *or* **abii, abitum**	go away
abstineo, abstinere, abstinui, abstentum	hold back, keep off
***ac**	and
accendo, accendere, accendi, accensum	kindle, set on fire, light
***accipio, accipere, accepi, acceptum**	receive
accubo, accubere, accubui, accubitum	lie down; sleep with
***acer, acris, acre**	severe, fierce, eager
acervus -i, m	heap, pile
Achilles, Achillis, m	Achilles
***acies, aciei, f**	line of battle, battle-array
acutus -a -um	sharp, clear
***ad (+ accusative)**	to; by, next to, beside
addisco, addiscere, addidici	learn in addition
***addo, addere, addidi, additum**	add, add to
adeo, adire, adii, aditum	reach, approach
adfecto, adfectare, adfectavi, adfectatum	aspire to, strive after, pursue, endeavour to make one's own
adfixus -a -um	intent on

admitto, admittere, admisi, admissum	commit
admoveo, admovere, admovi, admotum	move to
adoperio, adoperire, adoperui, adopertum	cover
adsideo, adsidere, adsedi, adsessum	sit by, be at one's side, attend, be busily engaged in
adsidue	continually, constantly, without intermission
adsiduus -a -um	constant, unremitting, incessant
*adsum, adesse, adfui	be present, come
*adversus -a -um	adverse, hostile
aedes, aedis, f	house; temple
Aegeus -a -um	Aegean
aeger, aegra, aegrum	ill, sick, unwell
*aequus -a -um	calm
aeratus -a -um	made of bronze
aes, aeris, n	brass
aestivus -a -um	(pertaining to) summer
aetas, aetatis, f	old age
agedum	come then
*ager, agri, m	field
agna -ae, f	ewe lamb
agnosco, agnoscere, agnovi, agnotum	recognize
*ago, agere, egi, actum	do, deal with
agrestis, agrestis, m	rustic, countryman
agricola -ae, m	farmer
ait	she says, she said
ala -ae, f	wing
aliqui, aliqua, aliquod	some, any

*alius, alia, aliud	other
*alter, altera, alterum	another, other
amarus -a -um	bitter
ambitiosus -a -um	ambitious, conceited
amens, amentis	out of one's mind, mad
*amica -ae, f	girlfriend
*amicus -i, m	friend
amnis, amnis, m	river, stream
*amo, amare, amavi, amatum	love
*amor, amoris, m	love
*an	or
*ancilla -ae, f	slave-girl, maid
Andromede, Andromedes, f	Andromeda
anguis, anguis, m	snake, serpent
*animus -i, m	mind, heart
annuo, annuere, annui, annutum	nod to, give assent
*annus -i, m	year; season
*ante (+ accusative)	before, in front of
ante	before, beforehand, first
antiquus -a -um	ancient
antrum -i, n	cave, grotto, glen
anus, anus, f	old woman
anxius -a -um	distressed, troubled, anxious
Aonius -a -um	Aonian
Apidanus -i, m	(River) Apidanus
appono, apponere, apposui, appositum	set beside
aptus -a -um	suited, serviceable, satisfactory
*aqua -ae, f	water
*arbor, arboris, f	tree
Arcadius -a -um	Arcadian

arcus, arcus, m	bow
ardeo, ardere, arsi, arsum	burn, be on fire, blaze; love
ardor, ardoris, m	fire, flame; passion
arguo, arguere, argui, argutum	plead one's case; accuse, charge with, argue
Argus -i, m	Argus
*arma -orum, n pl	arms, weapons
*ars, artis, f	art, skill, craft, stratagem
arvum -i, n	plough-land
asellus -i, m (diminutive of asinus)	a little donkey
aspicio, aspicere, aspexi, aspectum	look at, see
assiduus -a -um = adsiduus	
assuesco, assuescere, assuevi, assuetum	become familiar, accustom oneself to
Assyrius -a -um	Assyrian
*at	but
ater, atra, atrum	black, dark
*atque	and
Atrida -ae, m	son of Atreus
attenuo, attenuare, attenuavi, attenuatum	weaken, lessen, make slight
*audeo, audere, ausum sum	dare
*audio, audire, audivi *or* audii, auditum	hear, listen to
auris, auris, f	ear
auritus -a -um	long-eared
Aurora -ae, f	Dawn (the goddess of dawn)
aurum -i, n	gold
auspicium -ii, n	omen, sign
Auster, Austri, m	South wind

*aut	or
aut . . . aut	either . . . or
*auxilium -ii, n	help, aid; remedy
avidus -a -um	greedy
avis, avis, f	bird
avus -i, m	grandfather, forefather, ancestor

Bacchus -i, m	Bacchus; wine
bello, bellare, bellavi, bellatum	wage war
*bellum -i, n	war
*bene	well
benignus -a -um	rich, fruitful, fertile
bidens, bidentis, m	(two-pronged) mattock, hoe
*bis	twice
blanditia -ae, f	blandishment
*bona -orum, n pl	property
*bonus -a -um	good
bos, bovis, m	ox
Briseis, Briseidos, f	Briseis

*cado, cadere, cecidi, casum	fall; die
caecus -a -um	blind
*caedes, caedis, f	slaughter, carnage
caedo, caedere, cecidi, caesum	kill
*caelum -i, n	sky, heaven
caeruleus -a -um	blue-green
*campus -i, m	field
candidus -a -um	white, dazzling, bright, beautiful
*Canis, Canis, m	Dog-star, Sirius
*cano, canere, cecini, cantum	sing, compose (poetry)
canto, cantare, cantavi, cantatum	sing, enchant, bewitch

cantus, cantus, m	song, singing
canus -a -um	white, grey
capella -ae, f	she-goat
capillus -i, m	hair (of the head)
***capio, capere, cepi, captum**	catch, seize, lay hold of, capture
***caput, capitis, n**	head
careo, carere, carui, caritum	lack, be devoid of
carina -ae, f	keel; ship
carmen, carminis, n	song, poem, incantation
Carpathius -a -um	Carpathian
***carus -a -um**	dear, beloved
casia -ae, f	a tree with an aromatic bark, probably the wild cinnamon
castus -a -um	chaste; respectable; faithful
casu (ablative of casus)	by chance
***causa -ae, f**	case
causor, causari, causatus sum	allege as reason, make a pretext of, pretend, plead
cavus -a -um	hollow, cupped; perforated, full of holes
***cedo, cedere, cessi, cessum**	recede
celebro, celebrare, celebravi, celebratum	often approach (with offerings), worship
***celer, celeris, celere**	swift, fast, quick
Cepheius -a -um	of Cepheus
Cerberus -i, m	Cerberus
Ceres, Cereris, f	Ceres
***certus -a -um**	certain, sure; settled, steady; fixed, prearranged
cervix, cervicis, f	neck
chorea -ae, f	a dance (in a ring)
cingo, cingere, cinxi, cinctum	bind, wreathe

cinis, cineris, m	ashes
circa	around
circum	around
*circum (+ accusative)	around
*clamo, clamare, clamavi, clamatum	shout
classicum -i, n	(military) trumpet
claudo, claudere, clausi, clausum	close, shut, lock
Cnosius -a -um	Cnosian, of Cnossos
*cogito, cogitare, cogitavi, cogitatum	think, think up; with *in* + accusative: be disposed towards
*cognosco, cognoscere, cognovi, cognitum	become thoroughly acquainted, know
*cogo, cogere, coegi, coactum	force, compel
*cohors, cohortis, f	company of soldiers, division of an army, cohort, bodyguard of a general
colligo, colligere, collegi, collectum	recall
*colo, colere, colui, cultum	cultivate, tend; revere, worship, celebrate; adorn, ornament
color, coloris, m	colour; complexion
coloro, colorare, coloravi, coloratum	colour, tinge
columna -ae, f	column, pillar
colus, colus, f	distaff
coma -ae, f	hair
communis, commune	common, shared
como, comere, compsi, comptum	comb, do *or* dress (hair)

compendium -ii, n	profit, gain
compono, componere,	form, shape; store away
composui, compositum	
compositus -a -um	stored away; closed, sealed,
	settled at rest; lulled to sleep
	by wine, drowsy with wine
concido, concidere, concidi	fall down
concubitus -us, m	lying together, copulation
condicio, condicionis, f	terms
*condo, condere, condidi,	store up
conditum	
congero, congerere, congessi,	carry, bring together, collect,
congestum	heap up
*coniunx, coniugis, f	consort, wife
*conor, conari, conatus sum	try, attempt
conplector, conplecti,	embrace, clasp, hug
conplexus sum	
conscius -a -um	sharing in knowledge, aware,
	privy to, in the know;
	accomplice, confidant; guilty
conscribo, conscribere,	write all over, fill with writing
conscripsi, conscriptum	
*consilium -ii, n	sense, understanding
constans, constantis	steadfast
*consulo, consulere, consului,	consult, take counsel
consultum	
*consumo, consumere,	spend, consume, destroy, kill
consumpsi, consumptum	
contemero, contemerare,	pollute, defile
contemeravi	
contemno, contemnere,	despise, disdain, scorn, defy
contempsi, contemptum	

*contendo, contendere, contendi, contentum	contend, maintain, assert
contentus -a -um	contented, satisfied, content
contineo, continere, continui, contentum	hold tight
contingo, contingere, contigi, contactum	touch, seize (upon), take hold of, affect; hit; infect; + dative: happen to *or* befall one, be one's lot, come to pass for one
contundo, contundere, contudi, contusum	crush; subdue
conubium -ii, n	marriage; union
convenio, convenire, conveni, conventum	fit with, suit; be suitable, appropriate, proper; be harmonious, accord
converto, convertere, converti, conversum	change
conviva -ae, m/f	guest
cor, cordis, n	heart
Corinna -ae, f	Corinna
cornu, cornus, n	horn
corolla -ae, f (diminutive of corona)	little garland
corona -ae, f	crown, garland
*corpus, corporis, n	body
*corripio, corripere, correpi, correptum	seize
cotes, cotis, f	rock, crag, cliff
credibilis, credibile	to be believed, likely, credible
*credo, credere, credidi, creditum	believe, trust, have faith in
credulus -a -um	credulous, (easily) believing

*crimen, criminis, n	judgement, verdict; charge, accusation; crime, fault, offence, transgression
crinis, crinis, m	hair
cruentus -a -um	blood-stained, bloody
cubitum -i, n	elbow
cubo, cubare, cubui, cubitum	lie in bed
*culpa -ae, f	fault
culpo, culpare, culpavi, culpatum	reproach, blame, find fault with
*cum	when; whenever
*cum (+ ablative)	with
*cunctus -a -um	all (together)
Cupido, Cupidinis, m	Cupid
*cupidus -a -um	desirous, greedy
*cur	why
*cura -ae, f	care, object of care; cure; sweetheart
*curo, curare, curavi, curatum	care about, care for
*curro, currere, cucurri, cursum	run
currus, currus, m	chariot
cuspis, cuspidis, f	point; spear
*custos, custodis, m	guardian, sentry
Cynthia -ae, f	Cynthia
Cypassis, Cypassidis, f	Cypassis
Cytherea -ae, f	Cytherea, Cytherean (Venus)
Cytinaeus -a -um	of Cytina
Daedalius -a -um	Daedalian, of Daedalus
Danaus -i, m	Danaus
Dardanius -a -um	Dardanian, Trojan

*de (+ ablative)	from, of
*dea -ae, f	goddess
*debeo, debere, debui, debitum	owe, be bound to, have to
decenter	becomingly, in a way that becomes *or* suits
decet, decuit (impersonal)	it is becoming, it suits, it is seemly, it behooves
*deceptus -a -um	disguised, camouflaged
dedo, dedere, dedidi, deditum	deliver up, surrender; impart, devote, give
deduco, deducere, deduxi, deductum	draw down, draw off
*defendo, defendere, defendi, defensum	defend
defero, deferre, detuli, delatum	carry off; bestow, award, confer
deficio, deficere, defeci, defectum	desert, forsake, fail, cease
defigo, defigere, defixi, defixum	fix, turn intently
defio, defieri = deficio	
deicio, deicere, deieci, deiectum	cast down
Delia -ae, f	Delia
delinquo, delinquere, deliqui, delictum	commit a misdemeanour
demitto, demittere, demisi, demissum	cast down, bow
deperdo, deperdere, deperdidi, deperditum	destroy, ruin, lose
desero, deserere, deserui, desertum	leave, forsake, abandon, leave behind
despicio, despicere, despexi, despectum	look down on, despise, disdain

destituo, destituere, destitui, destitutum	desert
deterior, deterius	worse, poorer
deterreo, deterrere, deterrui, deterritum	keep from, deter from
*deus -i, m	god
devinco, devincere, devici, devictum	conquer completely, subdue
Diana -ae, f	Diana
*dico, dicere, dixi, dictum	say, speak, call
dicto, dictare, dictavi, dictatum	dictate, suggest, order
*dies, diei, f	day
digitus -i, m	finger
*dignus -a -um	worthy
dimico, dimicare, dimicavi, dimicatum	contend, fight
*dirus -a -um	evil, ill-boding
dis, ditis	rich, wealthy
*discedo, discedere, discessi, discessum	leave, depart
dissimulo, dissimulare, dissimulavi, dissimulatum	dissemble, hide, cover up
diva -ae, f	goddess
diverto, divertere, diverti, diversum	part
*dives, divitis	rich, wealthy
*divitiae -arum, f pl	riches, wealth
divus -i, m	god
*do, dare, dedi, datum	give, administer, offer, provide; promise, foretell
*doceo, docere, docui, doctum	teach, tell, proclaim
doctus -a -um	learned, skilled

*doleo, dolere, dolui, dolitum	be pained, be distressed, be grieved, resent
dolium -ii, n	(very large) jar
*dolor, doloris, m	pain, distress, affliction, indignation, resentment
*domina -ae, f	mistress
*dominus -i, m	master, lord
dominus -a -um	sovereign, of a master
domo, domare, domui, domitum	tame; overcome, subdue
*domus, domus, f	home, house, town-house
donec	until
*donum -i, n	gift
*dormio, dormire, dormivi *or* dormii, dormitum	sleep
*duco, ducere, duxi, ductum	lead; lead aside, divert; draw out, mould, forge; draw, heave
dulce	sweetly
dulcis, dulce	sweet
Dulichia -ae, f	Dulichium; Ithaca
*dum (+ indicative)	while
*dum (+ subjunctive)	as long as; until
dum modo	provided that, if only
duplex, duplicis	double, twofold
*durus -a -um	hard, harsh, unfeeling
*dux, ducis, m	leader, guide, commander
*e, ex (+ ablative)	out, out of, of, from
ebrius -a -um	drunk, intoxicated
ebur, eboris, n	ivory
ecce	look!
edo, edere, edidi, editum	give out, put forth, produce

Edonis, Edonidis, f	Edonian woman; Bacchant
educo, educare, educavi, educatum	bring to maturity
effundo, effundere, effudi, effusum	let down, loosen; billow
***ego**	I
***egredior, egredi, egressus sum**	go out, leave, set out
ei	oh!
Electra -ae, f	Electra
eligo, eligere, elegi, electum	pick out, choose, elect
Elysius -a -um	Elysian
emereo, emerere, emerui, emeritum	gain the favour of
emodulor, emodulari	set to rhythm, measure off in song, celebrate in rhythm
en	look!
ensis, ensis, m	sword
***eo, ire, ii** *or* **ivi, itum**	go, walk, move; attack
***equus -i, m**	horse
***ergo**	therefore, so
***erro, errare, erravi, erratum**	wander
error, erroris, m	wandering
erubesco, erubescere, erubui	redden, blush
***et**	and; too
***etiam**	and now, and also, besides, and even, and yet
exclamo, exclamare, exclamavi, exclamatum	cry out, shout out, exclaim
excubo, excubare, excubui, excubitum	lie out on guard, keep watch, guard
excutio, excutere, excussi, excussum	to shake off, wrest from one's hands

exerceo, exercere, exercui, exercitum	exercise, train; harry, torment
exigo, exigere, exegi, exactum	drive out; conclude
exiguus -a -um	meagre, little, small
***exitium -ii, n**	ruin, destruction
expello, expellere, expuli, expulsum	throw out, expel
experior, experiri, expertus sum	experience
expleo, explere, explevi, expletum	complete, fill
externus -a -um	foreign, strange, of another
extremus -a -um	furthest, furthermost
exuviae -arum, f pl	spoils (of war)
fabella -ae, f (diminutive of fabula)	a brief narrative, a short fable, tale, story
faber, fabri, m	craftsman, smith
facies, faciei, f	face, appearance, beauty
***facilis, facile**	easy, favourable, ready; expert, practised, nimble; easy to handle, malleable; susceptible to, open to, compliant
***facio, facere, feci, factum**	do, make, cause
factum -i, n	doing, deed; misdeed
fallacia -ae, f	trick
***fallo, fallere, fefelli, falsum**	deceive, trick, cheat
falsus -a -um	pretended, supposed
falx, falcis, f	pruning hook
fames, famis, f	hunger, famine
famula -ae, f	slave-girl, maid

fastus -us, m	pride, scorn
fateor, fateri, fassus sum	confess
fatalis, fatale	fated
fatum -i, m	fate
***faveo, favere, favi, fautum**	be favourable, be well disposed,
(+ dative)	protect
fax, facis, f	torch
***felix, felicis**	prosperous; happy
***femina -ae, f**	woman
fenestra -ae, f	window shutter
fera -ae, f	wild beast, wild animal
***fero, ferre, tuli, latum**	carry, bear, offer, give, bring, deal,
	take; accept an offering,
	receive; suffer
ferreus -a -um	made of iron
***ferrum -i, n**	iron
ferus -a -um	savage, fierce
fessus -a -um	tired, worn out
fetus, fetus, m	young, offspring
fictile, fictilis, n	earthenware vessel
fictilis, fictile	made of clay, earthen
***fides, fidei, f**	belief, faith, trust
fidus -a -um	faithful, trustworthy, trusty
figo, figere, fixi, fixum	fix, fasten, transfix, set
fingo, fingere, finxi, fictum	fabricate, invent
finis, finis, m	boundary
flaveo, flavere	be golden yellow
flavesco, flavescere	become yellow
flavus -a -um	golden, blond
fleo, flere, flevi, fletum	weep, mourn, cry
floreo, florere, florui	flower, bloom
floridus -a -um	of flowers, flowery, blooming

*flumen, fluminis, n	river, stream
focus -i, m	hearth, fire-place
foris, foris, f	door
formo, formare, formavi, formatum	fashion, shape, compose, arrange
formosus -a -um	beautiful
*forte	by chance
*fortis, forte	strong
fortiter	bravely; with strength, powerfully
*frango, frangere, fregi, fractum	break, smash
*frater, fratris, m	brother
frequens, frequentis	in great numbers
freni -orum, m pl	bit
frigidus -a -um	cool, sexually unresponsive
frons, frontis, f	forehead, brow
fructus, fructus, m	produce, harvest
*frustra	in vain, mistakenly
frux, frugis, f	fruit, crops
*fugio, fugere, fugi, fugitum	flee, escape
fugo, fugare, fugavi, fugatum	put to flight, rout
fulgeo, fulgere, fulsi	glitter, gleam, shine
fulvus -a -um	yellow
fundo, fundere, fudi, fusum	pour, pour out
fur, furis, m	thief
*furor, furoris, m	madness, rage, fury, frenzy
furtive	stealthily, furtively
furtivus -a -um	stolen, stealthy, furtive
furtum -i, n	theft, deceit; stolen *or* secret love, intrigue
fuscus, -a -um	dark, swarthy, dusky

*gaudeo, gaudere, gavisus sum	rejoice, take pleasure in
*gaudium -ii, n	joy, delight, pleasure
gelidus -a -um	icy cold, freezing, icy
gena -ae, f	cheek
gens, gentis, f	people, nation, race
genu, genus, n	knee
germana -ae, f	(full) sister
*gero, gerere, gessi, gestum	carry, bear, wear
grandis, grande	large, tall, substantial
gratus -a -um	beloved, dear, pleasing; favoured
*gravis, grave	heavy, weighty
grex, gregis, f	herd
guttur, gutturis, n	gullet, throat
*habeo, habere, habui, habitum	have
hac	this way
haereo, haerere, haesi, haesum	stand still, cling, hold fast, stick
Heliconius -a -um	Heliconian
herbosus -a -um	grassy
*heri	yesterday
heu	ah, alas
hibernus -a -um	wintry
*hic	here, over here
*hic, haec, hoc	this
hirsutus -a -um	rough, shaggy, bristly
*hodie	today
*hora -ae, f	hour
*hortus -i, m	here, orchard; more generally, garden
hostia -ae, f	victim, sacrifice, sacrificial victim
hostilis, hostile	(belonging to an) enemy

*hostis, hostis, m	enemy
*huc	hither, to this place
Hylaeus -a -um	of Hylaeus
*iaceo, iacere, iacui	lie
*iam	now, already; still; soon
ianitor, ianitoris, m	door-keeper
Iasis, Iasidos, f	daughter of Iasius (Atalanta)
*ignis, ignis, m	fire
ignotus -a -um	unfamiliar, unrecognized, strange, unknown
*ille, illa, illud	he/she/it; that
*illic	there, in that place
illuc	thither, to that place
immisceo, immiscere, immiscui, immixtum	mix in, intermingle, join, unite with
immitis, immite	harsh, severe, savage, ungentle; unripe, untimely, premature
immortalis, immortale	immortal
impello, impellere, impuli, impulsum	push over
*impetus -us, m	impulse, passion
impexus -a -um	uncombed, unkempt
impius -a -um	impious, wicked
impono, imponere, imposui, impositum	put upon, place on, impose
imprimo, imprimere, impressi, impressum	press on
improbus -a -um	no good, wicked, shameless, impudent
*in (+ accusative)	into; towards; against
*in (+ ablative)	in, on

Inachis, Inachidos, f	daughter of Inachus
incolumis, incolume	unhurt, uninjured, safe
increpo, increpare, increpui, increpitum	reprimand, rebuke
index, indicis, m/f	informer
indicium -ii, n	informing
ineo, inire, inii *or* inivi, initum	enter into
iners, intertis	inactive, quiet, unwarlike, idle
infelix, infelicis	unfortunate, unhappy, miserable
inferus -a -um	lower
ingemo, ingemere, ingemui	groan, wail, lament
ingratus -a -um	ungrateful, thankless
*ingredior, ingredi, ingressus sum	embark on
inicio, inicere, inieci, iniectum	lay on
*iniquus -a -um	unfair
*iniuria -ae, f	offence, violation, scorn, rejection
innumerus -a -um	countless
inprobus -a -um = improbus	
insanus -a -um	mad, insane
inscribo, inscribere, inscripsi, inscriptum	write on, inscribe
insero, inserere, inserui, insertum	introduce, insert, begin
*insignis, insigne	notable, outstanding, distinguished
insimulo, insimulare, insimulavi, insimulatum	make a charge against, make an allegation
insolitus -a -um	unusual
*instruo, instruere, instruxi, instructum	furnish, provide, equip, fit out with

intendo, intendere, intendi, intentum	strain
*inter (+ accusative)	in the midst, in between, between
*interea	meanwhile, until then
interdum	occasionally, now and then
*invitus -a -um	against one's will
io	io (a ritual exclamation)
*ipse, ipsa, ipsum	self
*ira -ae, f	anger
*iratus -a -um	angry
Isis, Isidis, f	Isis
iste, ista, istud	this, that
*ita	so, thus
*iter, itineris, n	way, journey, path, route
*iubeo, iubere, iussi, iussum	order, command, make (to do something)
iucundus -a -um	pleasant
iugerum -i, n	acre
iugosus -a -um	mountainous
iugum -i, n	yoke
*iungo, iungere, iunxi, iunctum	join, unite, associate; exchange
Iuno, Iunonis, f	Juno
Iuppiter, Iovis, m	Jupiter
iurgium -i, n	railing, quarrel
iuro, iurare, iuravi, iuratum	swear, take an oath
ius, iuris, n	right
*iuvenis, iuvenis, m	young man
*iuvo, iuvare, iuvi, iutum	help, help along
iuvat (impersonal)	it pleases, it delights, it is pleasant
iuvencus -i, m	young bull, steer

Ixion, Ixionis, m	Ixion
labellum -i, n (diminutive of labrum)	a little lip
*labor, labi, lapsus sum	fall, slip down, slip
*labor, laboris, m	work, toil, exertion
*laboro, laborare, laboravi, laboratum	toil, labour, strive, suffer, labour under
lac, lactis, n	milk
lacertus -i, m	upper arm
lacrima -ae, f	tear
lacus, lacus, m	vat, basin, tank, cistern; pond, lake
*laedo, laedere, laesi, laesum	harm, hurt, injure, offend
laetor, laetari, laetatus sum	rejoice, be glad
languidus -a -um	languid, limp, exhausted
lanio, laniare, laniavi, laniatum	tear, mangle, lacerate
Laomedon, Laomedontis, m	Laomedon
lapis, lapidis, m	stone
Lar, Laris, m	Lar
largior, largiri, largitus sum	bestow, lavish
*laudo, laudare, laudavi, laudatum	praise
*laus, laudis, f	praise
lavo, lavare, lavi, lautum	wash
lectus -i, m	bed, couch
*lego, legere, legi, lectum	collect, gather; choose, pick out
*lentus -a -um	unmoved, indifferent; clinging; relaxed; slow, long-lasting
Letheus -a -um	of Lethe
letum -i, n	death

levo, levare, levavi, levatum	lighten, relieve, ease, rest
*levis, leve	light, carefree, fickle, changeable
leviter	lightly, slightly
*lex, legis, f	rule
Liber, Liberi, m	Liber, Bacchus
*liber, libera, liberum	free
*libertas, libertatis, f	freedom, liberty
libido, libidinis, f	desire, eagerness, inclination
libo, libare, libavi, libatum	put out as an offering
*licet, licuit, licitum est (impersonal)	it is allowed
lilium -ii, n	lily
lingua -ae, f	tongue
linum -i, n	linen; linen thread
liqueo, liquere, liqui *or* licui	be clear
litoreus -a -um	of the shore, from the shore
*littera -ae, f	letter
*litus, litoris, n	shore
*locus -i, m	place
*longus -a -um	long
*loquor, loqui, locutus sum	speak, say
luceo, lucere, luxi	shine, be clear; glow
lucerna -ae, f	lamp, oil-lamp
Lucifer, Luciferi, m	the Morning-star (the planet Venus), Light-bringer, day
ludo, ludere, lusi, lusum	play
lumen, luminis, n	light; eye
luna -ae, f	moon
luno, lunare, lunavi, lunatum	bend like a half-moon, arch
lupus -i, m	wolf
lustro, lustrare, lustravi, lustratum	purify (by means of an offering)

lutum -i, n	clay
*lux, lucis, f	light; dear
lyra -ae, f	lyre
Maeonis, Maeonidis, f	Maeonian, Lydian
maestus -a -um	sad, (connected with) mourning, funerary
magicus -a -um	magical
*magis	more
*magister, magistri, m	teacher, master
*magnus -a -um	great
maior, maius (comparative of magnus)	greater
malum -i, n	bad thing, evil, mischief, misfortune, harm, wrong-doing, torment
*malus -a -um	bad, poor
mandatum -i, n	parting instruction
manes, manium, m pl	spirit of the dead, departed spirit, shade
*manus, manus, f	hand
*mare, maris, n	sea
marmoreus -a -um	made of marble
Mars, Martis, m	Mars
Martius -a -um	belonging to Mars, martial, military
*mater, matris f	mother
materia -ae, f	subject matter, material
maturus -a -um	timely, seasonable, of the proper age
maximus -a -um (superlative of magnus)	very great, greatest

medeor, mederi	heal, cure
medicina -ae, f	medicine, remedy
*medius -a -um	middle of, mid
mel, mellis, n	honey
melior, melius (comparative of bene)	better
membrum -i, n	limb
memini, meminisse	remember, recollect, think of
memor, memoris (+ genitive)	remembering, mindful
*mens, mentis, f	mind
mensa -ae, f	table
menstruus -a -um	monthly
mereo, merere, merui, meritum	deserve, earn
merum -i, n	unmixed wine, wine not mixed with water
merx, mercis, f	merchandise, wares, goods
Messalla -ae, m	Messalla
messis, messis, f	crops, harvest
metuo, metuere, metui, metutum	fear, be afraid
*meus -a -um	my, mine
Milanion, Milanionis, m	Milanion
*miles, militis, m	soldier
militia -ae, f	military service, campaign, warfare
mille	thousand
Minerva -ae, f	Minerva
ministra -ae, f	female attendant, maid-servant, assistant
Minois, Minoidis, f	daughter of Minos
minus	less

misceo, miscere, miscui, mixtum	mix, mingle
*miser, misera, miserum	pitiable, wretched, poor
miserandus -a -um	pitiable, deplorable
*mitto, mittere, misi, missum	send, let go, let leave
*modo	only, just, just now; if only
*modo ... modo	now ... now, at one moment ... at another
*modus -i, m	metre, rhythm; way
mollis, molle	soft, gentle, compliant, yielding
molliter	softly, gently
moneo, monere, monui, monitum	advise, admonish, warn
monitum -i, n	advice, admonition
*mora -ae, f	delay
mordeo, mordere, momordi, morsum	bite, chew, champ
*morior, mori, mortuus suum	die
*moror, morari, moratus sum	detain, delay, linger
*mors, mortis, f	death
motus, motus, m	movement, motion
*moveo, movere, movi, motum	move, stir, set in motion; play (an instrument); wage (war)
*multus -a -um	much, many
*munus, muneris, n	gift
Musa -ae, f	Muse
mustum -i, n	new wine
*muto, mutare, mutavi, mutatum	change
Mycenaeus -a -um	Mycenaean, from Mycenae
myrteus -a -um	of myrtle

myrtum -i, n	myrtle
***nam**	for (conjunction)
***narro, narrare, narravi, narratum**	tell, report
***nascor, nasci, natus sum**	be born
***navis, navis, f**	ship
***navita -ae, m**	sailor
***ne**	lest, that; that not; not
ne quis	if anyone
***nec**	and not, nor
necto, nectere, nexui, nexum	bind, tie, fasten, join, fasten together, connect
***nego, negare, negavi, negatum**	say no, refuse
***nemo, neminis, m/f**	no one
neque	and not
nervus -i, m	sinew, nerve, vigor, power
nescioquis	someone, I don't know who
neu, neve	nor, or that (not), and not, and that (not)
niger, nigra, nigrum	black, dark
nimium	too, too much, exceedingly
***nisi**	if not, unless
niteo, nitere	shine, gleam, be bright, be beautiful
nitor, niti, nixus sum	lean, rest on
***nomen, nominis, n**	name
***non**	not
***nondum**	not yet
***nos**	we
***nosco, noscere, novi, notum**	get to know; (perfect) know

*noster, nostra, nostrum	our, ours
nota -ae, f	mark, sign, note, signal, letter, code; mark on a wine-cask (to denote the quality of the wine); sort, kind, quality
Notus -i, m	South wind
novem	nine
*novus -a -um	new
*nox, noctis, f	night
noxius -a -um	harmful, injurious, noxious; guilty, criminal
nudo, nudare, nudavi, nudatum	bare; expose, lay bare
*nullus -a -um	no, not any, none
*num	question word expecting the answer no: surely . . . not?
numen, numinis, n	godhead, divine spirit
*numerus -i, m	rhythm, metre, (metrical) foot
*numquam	never
*nunc	now
*nuntio, nuntiare, nuntiavi, nuntiatum	announce
nusquam	on no occasion, not at all
nutus, nutus, m	nod, nodding

o	o
*ob (+ accusative)	on account of
obicio, obicere, obieci, obiectum	bring as a charge
*obliviscor, oblivisci, oblitus sum	forget, be forgetful
obstupesco, obstupescere, obstupui	be dumbstruck

obvius -a -um (+ dative)	in the way, to meet
ocellus -i, m (diminutive of oculus)	a little eye, eyelet
*oculus -i, m	eye
*odi, odisse	hate
odor, odoris, m	perfume
odoratus -a -um	fragrant, sweet-smelling
offendo, offendere, offendi, offensum	hit against, dash against
*officium -ii, n	service, favour
omen, ominis, n	omen, sign
*omnis, omne	all, every, entire
onustus -a -um	freighted, loaded
operosus -a -um	painstaking in, meticulously attentive to
opes, opum, f pl	wealth, riches
oppono, opponere, opposui, oppositum	place before *or* against, oppose
optimus -a -um	best, very good
opto, optare, optavi, optatum	wish for, desire
*opus, operis, n	work, labour, task
Orestes, Orestis, m	Orestes
*orno, ornare, ornavi, ornatum	arrange, dress hair
Orpheus -a -um	of Orpheus, Orphean
ortus, ortus, m	rising
*os, oris, n	mouth, face
os, ossis, n	bone
osculum -i, n (diminutive of os)	little mouth; kiss
ovis, ovis, f	sheep, ewe
pagina -ae, f	page
Pales, Palis, f	Pales

palleo, pallere, pallui	be *or* look pale
palma -ae, f	palm
*par, paris	equal
*parco, parcere, peperci, parsum (+ dative)	spare
*paro, parare, paravi, paratum	prepare
*pars, partis, f	part, portion
Parthenius -a -um	Parthenian, belonging to Mount Parthenius
Parthi -orum, m pl	Parthians
*parvus -a -um	small, little
pasco, pascere, pavi, pastum	feed, pasture
*passim	hither and thither
pastor, pastoris, m	shepherd
patefacio, patefacere, patefeci, patefactum	open, lay open
*pater, patris, m	father, forefather, ancestor
*patior, pati, passus sum	bear, undergo, suffer
patrius -a -um	of one's fathers, paternal, hereditary, family
*paulatim	gradually, little by little
*pauper, pauperis	poor
paupertas, paupertatis, f	poverty, humble means
peccatum -i, n	fault, transgression, crime
pecco, peccare, peccavi, peccatum	wrong, break against, offend
pectus, pectoris, n	chest, breast, heart
pecus, pecoris, n	flock
*pello, pellere, pepuli, pulsum	strike; call, blast
Penates, Penatium, m pl	Penates
pendeo, pendere, pependi	hang

pensum -i, n	wool weighed out for a day's spinning, allotment of wool
*per (+ accusative)	through, over; by
percutio, percutere, percussi, percussum	strike, hit, smite
perduco, perducere, perduxi, perductum	pass, spend (through)
*pereo, perire, perii, peritum	perish
perfectus -a -um	perfect, excellent, exquisite, very skilled
periurium -ii, n	a false oath, perjury
perpetuus -a -um	constant, unremitting, neverending
persolvo, persolvere, persolui, persolutum	fulfil
peruro, perurere, perussi, perustum	burn up, burn thoroughly, consume
*pes, pedis, m	foot
*peto, petere, petivi, petitum	seek, pursue, attack
Phaeacia -ae, f	Phaeacia
pharetra -ae, f	quiver
pharetratus -a -um	quiver-bearing, wearing a quiver
Pharius -a -um	Pharian, of Pharos; Alexandrian; Egyptian
Phoebas, Phoebadis, f	priestess of Phoebus, prophetess
Phoebus -i, m	Phoebus (epithet of Apollo)
pie	piously, dutifully
Pieris, Pieridis, f	daughter of Pieros, a Muse; Pierian
piget, piguit, pigitum est (impersonal)	it irks, it displeases, it disgusts
pingo, pingere, pinxi, pictum	paint

pinguis, pingue	rich
pinus, pinus, f	pine; pine-wood ship
pio, piare, piavi, piatum	appease, propitiate; perform rites
***placeo, placere, placui,** **placitum**	please, satisfy
placidus -a -um	appeased, kindly
***plenus -a -um**	full, brimming, laden
ploro, plorare, ploravi, **ploratum**	cry, lament
pluvia -ae, f	rain
poculum -i, n	cup
***poena -ae, f**	punishment
pomosus -a -um	full of fruit, abounding in fruit
pomum -i, n	fruit, apple; fruit-tree
pondus, ponderis, n	weight
***pono, ponere, posui, positum**	place, put, lay; set up; arrange
porrigo, porrigere, porrexi, **porrectum**	stretch out
***porta -ae, f**	gate, gateway (of the city), city-gate
***porto, portare, portavi,** **portatum**	bring, carry
***possum, posse, potui**	be able, can, may
postis, postis, m	doorpost
***potens, potentis**	powerful, mighty
potior, potius (comparative of **potis)**	preferable, greater
***potius**	rather
poto, potare, potavi, potatum **or potum**	drink
***praebeo, praebere, praebui,** **praebitum**	provide, offer, grant

praecordia -orum, n pl	heart, breast
praecurro, praecurrere, praecucurri, praecursum	run past
*praeda -ae, f	spoils, plunder, booty, prey
praefero, praeferre, praetuli, praelatum	carry before one, wear, sport
praeripio, praeripere, praeripui, praereptum	snatch away, carry off
praesens, praesentis	composed, collected
praetereo, praeterire, praeterii, praeteritum	pass, go by
*precor, precari, precatus sum	pray, entreat, beg
premo, premere, pressi, pressum	press, tread on; bear down on; weigh down
*pretium -ii, n	price
prex, precis, f	prayer, entreaty
Priapus -i, m	Priapus
primum	first, at first
*primus -a -um	first
*priusquam	before
*pro (+ ablative)	instead of, in lieu of, for, in return for
probo, probare, probavi, probatum	approve of, sanction
*procul	far away
proditor, proditoris, m	betrayer, traitor
*proelium -ii, n	battle
profundus -a -um	deep, vast, boundless
prohibeo, prohibere, prohibui, prohibitum	forbid
prosum, prodesse, profui	be useful, benefit, profit
proles, prolis, f	offspring, progeny, child

pronus -a -um	downward sloping
Propertius -ii, m	Propertius
protinus	at once, immediately
***proximus -a -um**	next
pubes, pubis, f	people
pudet, puduit, puditum est	it causes shame
(**impersonal**)	
***pudor, pudoris, m**	modesty, bashfulness, decency,
	shame, blush of shame
***puella -ae, f**	girl
***puer, pueri, m**	boy
pulcher, pulchra, pulchrum	beautiful
pulso, pulsare, pulsavi,	beat
pulsatum	
purpureus -a -um	purple, vermilion, scarlet
pure	purely, with ritual purity
purus -a -um	pure, clean, simple, unadorned,
	chaste
***puto, putare, putavi,**	think
putatum	
qua	where
***quaero, quaerere, quaesivi** *or*	seek, search for
quaesii, quaesitum	
quaeso, quaesere, quaesivi *or*	ask, beg
quaesii	
quale	how, in what way
qualis, quale	just as, such as
***quam**	how, how much, how greatly;
	than
quamvis	although, however much, as
	much as

quantum	as much as, however much
*quantus -a -um	how great, how much
quare	why
quatio, quatere, quassum	shake
*-que	and
quercus, quercus, f	oak
*queror, queri, questus sum	complain, lament
*qui, quae, quod	who, which
quicumque, quaecumque, quodcumque	whoever, whosoever, whatever, whichever
quid	what; why
*quidam, quaedam, quoddam	a certain, someone, something
*quidem	indeed
*quies, quietis, f	rest, repose
quin	that
quinque	five
*quis, quid	who? which? any, anyone, anybody, anything
*quisquam, quaequam, quicquam	any, any one
*quisque, quaeque, quodque	every, each one
*quod	because; that
*quod si	but if
quondam	once, at one time
*quoque	also, too
*quot	each, every; how many?
*quotiens	how often, how many times, as often as
radius -ii, m	ray
ramus -i, m	branch
rapax, rapacis	grasping, greedy, rapacious

rarus -a -um	rare, occasional
ratis, ratis, f	raft, bark, boat
rea -ae, f	(female) defendant
***recipio, recipere, recepi, receptum**	receive, accept
recordor, recordari, recordatus sum	think over, think about, call to mind
***reddo, reddere, reddidi, redditum**	render, give, give in return
reditus, reditus, m	return
***refero, referre, rettuli, relatum**	bring back, carry back; tell, report; remember, recall
***rego, regere, rexi, rectum**	direct, lead; rule, measure off
regno, regnare, regnavi, regnatum	reign
regnum -i, n	dominion, rule, authority; kingdom
***relinquo, relinquere, reliqui, relictum**	leave behind, quit
remaneo, remanere, remansi	stay behind, remain behind
remitto, remittere, remisi, remissum	relax, slacken
renuo, renuere, renui	nod back the head, deny by a motion of the head; refuse
repello, repellere, reppuli, repulsum	shake
rependo, rependere, rependi, repensum	pay back, repay, requite, reward
***repente**	suddenly
repeto, repetere, repetivi *or* repetii, repetitum	seek, bring back
repulsa -ae, f	rejection, refusal

requiesco, requiescere, requievi, requietum	rest
requiro, requirere, requisivi *or* **requisii, requisitum**	seek, require, need
resido, residere, resedi	settle down, fall
resolvo, resolvere, resolvi, resolutum	loosen, unbind
respicio, respicere, respexi, respectum	look back (at); look back *or* view *or* regard with alarm *or* anxiety *or* solicitude
*retineo, retinere, retenui, retentum	hold back
reus -i, m	(male) defendant
revoco, revocare, revocavi, revocatum	call back
*rex, regis, m	king
rideo, ridere, risi, risum	laugh, smile
rivus -i, m	stream, brook
rixa -ae, f	quarrel, row, brawl
*rogo, rogare, rogavi, rogatum	ask
rosa -ae, f	rose
roseus -a -um	rosy, rose-coloured
rota -ae, f	wheel
ruber, rubra, rubrum	red
rupes, rupis, f	rock, cliff
*rursus	(and) again
*rus, ruris, n	farm, estate
rusticus -a -um	rustic, of the country; simple, rough, boorish; countryman, country bumpkin
sacer, sacra, sacrum	sacred

sacra -orum, n pl	rites, rituals
***saepe**	often, repeatedly
saevio, saevire, saevii, saevitum	rage, be furious, rave
saevitia -ae, f	harshness, savageness, cruelty
***saevus -a -um**	harsh, savage, cruel, ferocious
sagitta -ae, f	arrow
salvus -a -um	safe, saved, unhurt, well
sanctus -a -um	sacred, inviolable, venerable, holy, sacrosanct
sanus -a -um	healthy, sane
***satis**	enough
Saturnus -i, m	Saturn
saucius -a -um	wounded
sceleratus -a -um	wicked, bad
scilicet	it is clear, clearly, obviously, of course, undoubtedly, to be sure
***scio, scire, scivi, scitum**	know
***se**	himself, herself, themselves
seco, secare, secui, sectum	cut, slash, wound
secubo, secubare, secubui	sleep apart, sleep by oneself
securus -a -um	carefree, at ease, at peace
***sed**	but
sedeo, sedere, sedi, sessum	sit
***sedes, sedis, f**	abode
sedulus -a -um	over-zealous, officious; persistent, busy, diligent, careful, unremitting
seges, segetis, f	crop; land, ground, soil
segnis, segne	cowardly, inactive, sluggish
semita -ae, f	path, way
***semper**	always

sensus, sensus, m	sense, faculty
*sentio, sentire, sensi, sensum	sense, feel; perceive, notice, find out; enjoy
sepulcrum -i, n	grave, tomb
*sequor, sequi, secutus sum	follow, pursue
series, seriem, serie, f	row, line, rank
sermo, sermonis, m	speech, conversation
sero	late, too late
sero, serere, sevi, satum	plant
serpens, serpentis, m/f	serpent, snake
serta -orum, n pl	garlands
serus -a -um	late
*servo, servare, servavi, servatum	save, keep unharmed
servus -a -um	servile, slave
*seu ... seu *or* sive	whether. .. or
severus -a -um	serious, strict, stern
sex	six
*si	if
*sic	so, in this way, in such a way, thus
siccus -a -um	dry
*sicut	so as, just as, as
sido, sidere, sidi	sink, settle, stick fast
sidus, sideris, n	star
*signum -i, n	military standard; sign
silex, silicis, m	flint
*silva -ae, f	forest, wood
*similis, simile	similar, like
*sine (+ ablative)	without
*sino, sinere, sivi, situm	allow, permit
sinuosus -a -um	bent, bending, pliant

sinus, sinus, m	fold, pocket, lap, bosom; embrace; dress; (fold of a) sail
sitis, sitis, f	thirst
***sive = seu**	
smaragdus -i, f	any bright green gem stone, e.g. emerald, beryl, jasper, malachite
sobrius -a -um	sober, not drunk
socio, sociare, sociavi, sociatum	join *or* unite together, associate
solator, solatoris, m	comforter, consoler
***soleo, solere, solitus sum**	be accustomed to, be in the habit of
solitus -a -um	customary, familiar
sollers, sollertis	skilled, skilful, crafty
solum -i, n	soil, land
***solus -a -um**	only, alone
***solvo, solvere, solvi, solutum**	loosen, take off; open, undo
***somnus -i, m**	sleep
sono, sonare, sonui, sonitum	make a sound, resound, sing
sopor, soporis, m	sleep
sordidus -a -um	lowly, base, uncouth
***soror, sororis, f**	sister
sors, sortis, f	lot; rank
spargo, spargere, sparsi, sparsum	sprinkle
***specto, spectare, spectavi, spectatum**	look upon, look at
***sperno, spernere, sprevi, spretum**	scorn, reject
***spes, spei, f**	hope
spiceus -a -um	of wheaten spikes, of ears of corn

spiculum -i, n (diminutive of spicum)	little sharp point; arrow
spiro, spirare, spiravi, spiratum	breathe, blow
*spolia -orum, n pl	spoils, booty, prey
sponsus -i, m	bridegroom
stagnum -i, n	pool, pond, swamp (of standing water)
stamen, staminis, n	thread, yarn
stimulus -i, m	goad
stipes, stipitis, m	stump (of a tree)
*sto, stare, steti, statum	stand; be
strideo, stridere, stridi	hiss
*stultus -a -um	foolish
*sub (+ ablative)	below, beneath, under
subeo, subire, subii, subitum	come *or* go under, bend under
subicio, subicere, subieci, subiectum	lay under, place under
subito	suddenly, of a sudden
subrepo, subrepere, subrepsi, subreptum	creep up
subrubeo, subrubere	be somewhat red *or* reddish, blush
succurro, succurrere, succurri, succursum (+ dative)	help, aid
sufficio, sufficere, suffeci, suffectum	be sufficient, suffice
*sum, esse, fui	be
*summus -a -um	topmost, highest, uppermost
*sumo, sumere, sumpsi, sumptum	snatch; take up
super (+ accusative)	above, on, over

supercilium -ii, n	eyebrow
supplex, supplicis, m	suppliant
supremus -a -um	last
surgo, surgere, surrexi, surrectum	rise, arise
surripio, surripere, surripui, surreptum	snatch
suspirium -ii, n	breath, sigh
*suus -a -um	his/her/their (own)
tabella -ae, f	tablet
taceo, tacere, tacui, tacitum	be silent
*talis, tale	such, just so
*tam	so
*tamen	nevertheless, however, yet, but
*tandem	at last, at length, finally
*tango, tangere, tetigi, tactum	touch, reach
Tantalides, Tantalidae, m	descendant of Tantalus (Agamemnon)
Tantalus -i, m	Tantalus
*tanti	worth so much
*tantum	so much, to such a degree; only
tardus -a -um	slow, sluggish; delaying, retarding, slowing; unpropitious
taurus -i, m	bull
*tego, tegere, texi, tectum	cover, veil
tellus, telluris, f	earth
*telum -i, n	weapon, missile, shaft
temere	rashly, thoughtlessly
tempe, n pl	valley
*templum -i, n	temple

tempto, temptare, temptavi, temptatum	touch, feel; make an attempt on; attack, assail
*tempus, temporis, n	time, season; temple (side of the head)
tenebrae -arum, f pl	darkness, shadows
*teneo, tenere, tenui, tentum	hold, own, occupy, detain
tener, tenera, tenerum	tender, delicate, soft; young
tenuis, tenue	slender, fine
tepidus -a -um	lukewarm, tepid
ter	three times, thrice
*tergum -i, n	back
*terra -ae, f	land, ground
*terreo, terrere, terrui, territum	frighten, terrify, scare
tertius -a -um	third
theatrum -i, n	theatre
Theseus, Theseos, m	Theseus
Theseus -a -um	of Theseus
Thessalus -a -um	Thessalian, from Thessaly
Tibullus -i, m	Tibullus
timidus -a -um	afraid, scared
*timor, timoris, m	terror, source of fear
tingo, tingere, tinxi, tinctum	dye, tinge
Tisiphone, Tisiphones, f	Tisiphone
Tithonus -i, m	Tithonus
Tityos, Tityi, m	Tityos
*tollo, tollere, sustuli, sublatum	draw
torqueo, torquere, torsi, tortum	torment, rack, torture
torus -i, m	bed, couch
totiens	so often, so many times
*totus -a -um	whole, entire, all
tracto, tractare, tractavi, tractatum	carry out, conduct, practise, exercise, handle

traduco, traducere, traduxi, traductum	transfer
***traho, trahere, traxi, tractum**	drag
trinus -a -um	each of three
***tristis, triste**	sad, gloomy, unlucky
trisulcus -a -um	triple, three-pronged
triumphus -i, m	triumph, triumphal procession
trivium -i, n	crossroads
***tu**	you (singular)
tuba -ae, f	trumpet
Tullus -i, m	Tullus
***tum**	then, at that time
tunc	then
***turba -ae, f**	crowd, crowd of followers, attendants
turbo, turbare, turbavi, turbatum	disturb; dishevel
turpis, turpe	unseemly, shameful, disgraceful
***tutus -a -um**	safe, secure, assured
tus, turis, n	incense, frankincense
***tuus -a -um**	your, yours (singular)
uber, uberis, n	udder, teat
***ubi**	where; when
***ubique**	everywhere
Ulixes, Ulixis, m	Odysseus
***ullus -a -um**	any
***ultimus -a -um**	last
ultro	of one's own accord, spontaneously; in contrast
umbra -ae, f	shadow, shade
***unda -ae, f**	wave

*unde	on account of whom; from whom
undeni -ae -a	eleven
unguis, unguis, m	nail, fingernail
unus -a -um	one
*urbs, urbis, f	city
uro, urere, ussi, ustum	burn, inflame
usquam	anywhere
*usque	always, constantly
*ut (+ indicative)	when, as, like
*ut (+ subjunctive)	in order to, to, that, so that; although; how
*uterque, utraque, utrumque	each (of two), both
utinam	if only, I wish that
vacuus -a -um	empty; idle, ineffectual
vadum -i, n	shallow, shoal
vagor, vagari, vagatus sum	wander, roam
vagus -a -um	roaming, wandering, vagabond
*valeo, valere, valui, valitum	have power, be effective, avail, be strong; fare well; stand for
*validus -a -um	strong
vanus -a -um	empty
vates, vatis, m	seer, prophet, poet
*-ve	or
velox, velocis	fast, quick, swift
veneror, venerari, veneratus sum	pray, revere, do homage
*venio, venire, veni, ventum	come; with *in* + accusative: become legally entitled to
ventilo, ventilare, ventilavi, ventilatum	brandish in the air, fan

*ventus -i, m	wind
Venus, Veneris, f	Venus; love
verber, verberis, n	whip, lash
*verbum -i, n	word
*vero	indeed, truly
verso, versare, versavi, versatum	turn *or* twist often *or* violently
versus, versus, m	verse, line
*vester, vestra, vestrum	your (plural)
vestibulum -i, n	entrance
vestigium -i, n	footstep, step
*veto, vetare, vetui, vetitum	deny, not allow, prevent
*vetus, veteris	old
*via -ae, f	path, road; travels
vibro, vibrare, vibravi, vibratum	tremble, shake, quiver, twitch
vicinus -a -um	nearby
*victoria -ae, f	victory
*video, videre, vidi, visum	see
*videor, videri, visus sum	seem, be seen, appear
vigeo, vigere	be lively, thrive, flourish
vilis, vile	worth little, paltry, cheap, worthless
vincio, vincire, vinxi, vinctum	bind, fetter
vinclum -i, n	fetter, chain
*vinco, vincere, vici, victum	win, vanquish, conquer
vinum -i, n	wine
violentus -a -um	violent, vehement, forcible
violo, violare, violavi, violatum	profane, desecrate
*vir, viri, m	man; husband; footsoldier
virgo, virginis, f	maiden
viscus, visceris, n	entrails, liver

*vita -ae, f	life
vitis, vitis, f	vine, grapevine
vitula -ae, f	young heifer
*vito, vitare, vitavi, vitatum	avoid, shun
*vivo, vivere, vixi, victum	live
*vix	scarcely, hardly
*voco, vocare, vocavi, vocatum	call
volatilis, volatile	flying, winged, flightly
*volo, velle, volui	want, wish
volvo, volvere, volvi, volutum	roll, tumble
*vos	you (plural)
votivus -a -um	vowed, votive
votum -i, n	vow, promise, wish, desire
*vox, vocis, f	voice, utterance; speech, word, language
*vulnus, vulneris, n	wound
*vultus, vultus, m	face